Writing is our Super Power

Inspired Ideas By Writing Rituals Collective

Ellen Coaty, Tim Crawford, Pam Daniel, Karen Fraase,
Jean Ferratier, Teri Freesmeyer, Keri Goble Billick,
Eva Hahn, Jean Hembrough, Nancy Hodge Long,
Kathy Jimerson, Sharron Magyar, John Malan,
Carlene Mattimore, Luna McGee, Megan McGee,
Michael Nelson, Bev Oberline, Don O'Neal,
Eden R. Souther, Ruth Souther, Marylynn Starling,
Diana Thornley, Terri Woodliff

Published by Crystal Heart Imprints, Springfield, IL
www.crystalheartimprints.com
Facebook: Crystal Heart Imprints
Interior: Keri Goble Billick
Cover Art: Sharron Magyar
Cover Design: Pam Daniel
Library of Congress Number: 2020901922
ISBN for Writing is Our Super Power: 978-1-945567-25-4
First Edition Printed in United States of America

Introduction

Writing Rituals began in 2007 because Terri Woodliff and I wanted a different kind of writing group – one that was supportive, generous, compassionate and encouraging to new authors.

We had both been involved in writing groups that were less than helpful, perhaps even mean-spirited when it came to the work of other authors. We were soon joined by Teri Freesmeyer, Sharron Magyar, Nancy Long, Sharon Stidham, Virginia Carlson, Brennan Stidham and Nicholas Schroeder. Sharon Stidham and Virginia Carlson have since moved away from the area, but all the others remain a dedicated group to providing a place for writers to create and share.

We have since been joined by Keri Goble Billick, and the entire list of authors who contributed to this book. We steadfastly honed our skills and now have 30 books out, or ready to be released under the umbrella of our publishing cooperative, Crystal Heart Imprints.

We are constantly creating, growing, and offering new workshops to keep our folks on their toes. As time passed, we realized our workshop writing exercises are wonderful pieces. We collected them, put them together in a document and went 'WOW.' That sparked the idea of a collaborative book with our local authors. In January of 2019, we put out the call for submissions, and lo and behold, received work from 24 authors!

Short stories, poetry, memoirs, book excerpts...the list goes on, all enchanting, funny, moving pieces. We are so proud of our writers! This group would not have continued for 13 years and counting if not for these talented and dedicated souls.

If you are a wannabe author, then these words are for you: Don't let anything or anyone stop you. There is support out there, and if not in your local area, start a group with the number one ground rule, be kind. We hope to make Writing is Our Super Power more than one volume, perhaps an annual thing. We also hope to put together all our trials and successes together in a book to guide other groups.

Until then, Superheroes, have courage and Write On!
Ruth Souther and the entire Writing Rituals group.
Facebook: writingrituals
Email: writingrituals@gmail.com

Table of Contents

Writing
Rituals
Exercises

Group Writing

Using 'Words of Truth' cards, the Writing Rituals Group wrote these snippets. We sent the pages around twice, once clockwise and then counterclockwise. The differences and sometimes the sameness were striking, and also fun.

Clockwise:

When my father left, the sense of abandonment was overwhelming. Life is a series of gifts, some beautiful and expected, some dark and unexpected. Humor is a stress reliever, a distraction at times, and an ice breaker that is understood in any language across the world.

As our velocity approached the speed of light, we broke through into what I call the dis-assemblage point, where upon Karla's face seemed to explode like fireworks before slowly reassembling to reassemble a serrate pointillist painting.

Speaking the truth often takes courage, no manipulation.

Life is magic! My life is in the absolute opposite of hopelessness and despair! I rarely feel anger. Although I will express it in the appropriate place. Often it comes out in my non-verbal communication.

The safety of my personal journal, where my temperament and imagination can unfold, allows me to begin tearing down the walls. The safety zone is no longer as safe, its struggling and the world is waiting for my authentic self. The tears fall more readily in flow and a new level of ecstasy is revealed.

As a writer, self-rejection becomes a stand-by emotion. Sometimes, the aggression to which I direct this rejection at myself is astonishing. In the end, though, I come back to the joy of creativity and the freedom of expression, the layers of emotion that range from the very darkest to sunlit inspiration to power my words.

Counterclockwise:

Some of the most interesting resolution come around thanks to non-verbal communications. No matter the time we must first find an appropriate place. Even anger is important when put where it needs to be.

Her excessive sensitivity manifested itself not only in her skin, but in her feelings, her emotions and her health. Even though I am female, I have no forbearance for those who can't take care of themselves. There I stood with a wish for immortality, therein lies my addiction to dissociation, and the fantasy bond with the creations of my mind.

At the assemblage point, Karla looked the same as I remembered her but, somehow, she seemed more beautiful than ever.

Humor can be offensive to some or all, depending on the content, but humor has a way of uniting all people if it is used properly. Life has a way of sneaking up on you, presenting options that have never occurred to you.

Abandonment is a crime against the sacred meaning of life, which is love. I find safety in the words that pour out onto the page, spilling from my imagined version of the story as a writer. I trepidatiously step into the world vulnerable as an author. My writer's family has my back and supports me with encouragement and yes, sometimes blunt force.

I believe in the joy of being alive! The intrinsic belief in the goodness of humanity drive me forward and is the basis of my life. Even though aggression and self-rejection is prevalent in society and politics, I hold onto the joy. I believe!

55 Word Stories

New Year's Resolutions

Ruth Souther

I admit that New Year's resolutions are like yesterday's socks, they have to be removed, laundered, folded and put away otherwise they become stinky, stiff and unresponsive to the shape of my feet. I need soft, pliable, breathable socks that move with me. Like goals, they should be flexible, supportive, and easy to change.

Joy and Appropriate Relationship

Keri Goble Billick

Creation is a living entity. It flows through and around us. We speak with it and listen to it. We have a relationship with it.

This relationship brings me joy. Expression, in words and images, comes from this relationship. For this I will be eternally grateful.

Dissociated Particles

Teri Freesmeyer

Gathering the pieces of dissociated particles of myself busy doing other things. So much pleasure to enjoy in the moment, in the world. So much to notice, touch and introduce myself too. Yet among them is all the other things I would rather be doing.

Repression

Sharron Magyar

Every day I work with people who have repressed thoughts and I believe repression is attached to something negative you are not prepared to handle. When I study the concept closer, I know many of those submerged emotions are the wellspring for my art and writing. Repression: yen and yang of life.

Tears/Essence

Nancy Hodge Long

Tears of joy flow easily as I see the essence of my being in each moment. Opening my heart brings awareness of others; their essence made of the exact same substance as mine. How is it I never saw this until now? Tears of joy flow in recognition that we are all One Creative Being.

A 55 word play

Tim Crawford

I am the Lord, thy God What?! Isn't that a fable? It is not
Well, I'm screwed. I have totally blasphemed. Not too late to repent
I don't have the energy
Do you hear yourself? I'm God and you're, like, I can't even I've got to get back to my Fortnite session.
Oh. My. God!

Generational patterns

Ellen Coaty

Because she dissociated from generational patterns, my freefall went undetected by my mother. She always thought I succeeded at life, not seeing how my failures mirrored hers. Still, I'd kept a roof over my head for twenty years, which was more than she did for me. You say I sound bitter? It's a family trait, I believe.

Letting Go and Guilt

Jean Ferratier

First described separately. Now I see a message.
Guilt equates to the, "I shoulds." Replace with a new chant.
"I get to."

Me Too

Michael Nelson

My Florence Nightingale is Aphrodite incarnate. She draws blood and handles urine samples all day.
I have never seen such perfect skin, such classical beauty. A compliment would surely give her day a boost.
An action is worth a thousand words. I gently touch her cheek.
Here I sit in county lockup rethinking life's choices.

Abundance

Don O'Neal

"Discussing abundance under these constraints will require patience, restraint, and a minimum of loquaciousness, but here goes:
Abundance may be negatively correlated with gratitude, as the less we have the more grateful we are for what we do have, whereas the more we have the more likely we are to take it for granted."

Out of the Gap

Pam Daniel

Becoming. As a professional I set my art down, for later. My inner artist slept. Awoken occasionally to express joy. It existed in gaps between thoughts and efforts to excel. I admit my breakthrough happened upon stripping away the planks of my avocation. Smiling, creativity welcomed me home.

Truckers Are Angels Too

Nancy Hodge Long

While driving on Route 4, I didn't realize my favorite ring was so loose that it flew out the window along with my apple core. After much searching, a semi stopped and the trucker stepped out, eyes set upon a specific spot, reaching for a small shining object. "Is this what you're looking for?"

What Writing Means To Me

What Writing Means To Me

Teri Freesmeyer

Freedom, exploration, contemplation and peace. Digging into cobwebs and chapters of the mind. Writing to me is an adventure into myself, my unseen thoughts and an entire universe or creative possibility. Short, long, rhyming, or jagged words are a dip into psychedelic paint. Where your palette mixes together one form with another and the result may be beautiful, muted, subtle or bold.

Writing means to me a pause in the outside world and a reset in the flow of life as my pen glides across the page. It means the greater I Am has something to say to my scattered bits to help find center again. Writing means I am remembering profound wisdom or humor I am transforming and allowing inspiration to override vulnerability about sharing my unique expression with others at the pleasure and release of serving myself this art. Writing is the gift of sharing what may impact another who needed my exact words that moment.

Writing offers a reunion of soul parts and a blueprint for goals. It offers words of encouragement, new perspectives and a chance to move energy from unformed into physical life. Writing offers me, the reader, escape, validation and entertainment. Writing offers me, the writer, fluidity and witness to the maturity of living life's hurdles and hopes into colorful and sensual memories.

Writing means freedom of expression and a fearlessness of self-acceptance.

What Writing Means To Me

Tim Crawford

How do I know what I think until I see what I say. —E.M. Forster
Not Me: What're you up to, Tim?

Me: Opening doors, making connections. Up here. (Points at head)
Not Me: Huh?

Me: Doing the creation thing. Writing. Not Me: Ah! You working on a new play?

Me: I'm not sure what this will be when it's put to paper or—

Not Me: Or other fixed form of expression to secure for a limited time copyright protection to promote science and the useful arts.

Me: Spoken like a copyright lawyer. You know what I value most about being a writer right now?

Not me: Hmm. What? Me: Identity.

Not Me: Okay...?

Me: I like having an identity aside from "retired guy." Don't get me wrong, I love retirement, but to most people it comes across as, I don't know, someone who has stopped having a purpose.

Not Me: I don't think that.

Me: Okay, not most people, but enough. As a writer, everything, every encounter has a purpose. It also makes my natural curiosity about people purposeful. You might remember this, from when we met: "What's your story?" is my favorite way to start a conversation with a stranger.

What Writing Means To Me

Jean Ferratier

First of all, there are so many types and purposes of writing. In any form it is about communication by me, and for me, and for others.

Writing is a way of remembering and helping to sort out, or make sense of jumbled thoughts.

At my most creative, it is a story, art form or poem of higher expression I wish to share.

A step below is wisdom to pass on or is a journal that serves as documentation; a scribe recording my life.

Then there are notes sent to convey sentiment or information to another.

On the practical plane, writing is my life line to memory; that which I need to know, but is the physical file sometimes more easily retrieved.

Finally, writing is my signature-the identifier of me; heart, mind, soul, and presence.

What Writing Means To Me

Jean Ferratier

I write because someday I may not remember.

What Writing Means To Me

Michael Nelson

Writing means freedom to me. I can unburden my mind from years' worth of accumulated thoughts and memories that no longer serve me. Cleaning the slate makes room for clearer thinking and creativity.

Journaling provides a sense of freedom that comes from exposing the bonds of limitations of the past. New clarity will appear in my mind. Since I am projecting into the future, I can only pray that this will be true. The current benefits are enough to keep me going.

Writing is a way to express myself and leave a record of what is going on with me. What I write for my children is part of my legacy. What I write for myself is self-expression that is for my pleasure, healing, and enlightenment.

There is much from the past I wish I had written what was going on at the time. Details start to fade and change as the years roll by. What something meant in the past may not have the same meaning. I will keep on writing so in the future I will have an accurate record of what is going on today.

What Writing Means To Me

By Eva Hahn

Writing means treasures I have found, shared and tucked away. My grandchildren are always asking me about stories their parents shared with them, and they want the details filled in. My children would ask their grandmother about things and she would tell the stories about her childhood. But no one wrote them down, so they faded and are gone with no one left to retrieve them.

Writing brings to mind things, people and incidents that have shaped me into who I am today. It gives me the opportunity to drag them out of the deep waters of the past, and walk around them and see parts and shades of color that I didn't see when I was in the midst and frenzy of the moment.

Writing something down allows me to go back and enjoy the glow of the story on a rainy afternoon. It is a legacy of where I have been; what I have walked through. Here I am.

Nature's Effect On My Day

Summer Affection

Pam Daniel

Golden rod and quaking aspen are glorious, but every hot August day they affect my life's experience. Their blooming makes my eyes itch, my sinus throb and cause me to stay inside in air-conditioned rooms. I enjoy natures beauty through my windows.

Nature's Effect On My Day

Jean Ferratier

From my bed each morning I gaze out the window. It is as automatic to me as breathing. Without consulting a clock, I gauge the approximate time of day. Sunrise is my favorite as the gorgeous hues of pink and yellow provide a backdrop for the silhouette of trees.

The tree out my window communicates the weather. I see the leaves blowing, rain dripping, sun reflections, branches packed with snow and sometimes ice crystals sparkling like diamonds in the sun.

Before I leave my bed the gaze out the window informs my mood, plans for the day, what I should wear. However, before leaving bed my gaze is the welcome and gratitude to the day.

Nature's Effect On My Day

Marylynn Starling

Nature has a tremendous effect on my day. I notice its effect most in the winter. Grey days have a big impact. Especially when there are many grey days piled up in a row. They have a pronounced gloomy effect on my mood and my outlook. I remember one winter in particular there were twenty-one (I counted) dreadfully grey days in succession. I remember yearning for even just a crack of sunshine in the sky. It made me feel heavy, like I was walking through a sticky sludge. This must be what depression feels like.

Nature's Effect On My Day

Karen Fraase

Beauty of the morning sky as the sun rises. Colors begin to shift into various vibrant shades. Shadow shapes move as the sun brightens the day. Gratitude fills my heart as the rays of sunshine beam inward. Baby blue with white puffs of clouds fill the sky— connecting to the higher grace. Fills my heart to step in to what my day may offer in gratitude and grace.

Nature's Effect On My Day

Ellen Coaty

Darn it, it's cloudy and looks like rain. My plans for a picnic with my grandson were likely to be washed out. I felt frustrated, having waited six weeks since my last visit with him and thought about what else I could do with a rambunctious six-year-old in tow. Something active, I thought, something fun.

When his stepmother dropped him off, she seemed to relish the weather turning my day askew. "So, no picnic today? Dylan will be so disappointed." Was that a smirk I saw on her face? I pushed those thoughts aside and replied, "Oh, we'll find something fun to do, won't we, Bud?" I tousled his hair and smiled. His dubious look told me I had better come up with something good.

No sooner had she left than thunder rumbled a warning of rain to come. I checked my weather app. Rain for the next 120 minutes it forecast. As if to prove the app correct, the sky opened, and a deluge poured from the clouds. "Come on, little Buddy." I grabbed Dylan's hand. "We're going to get wet!"

The summer shower was warm, and the rain soaked us through immediately. Large puddles formed in my driveway and I touched Dylan's shoulder and shouted, "Tag! You're it!" and dashed off. He followed me laughing through puddles and mud as we dashed around the yard.

When the rain stopped, we collapsed on the lawn, soaked with delight. "That was awesome, Gaga! Let's do it again!"

"Well, let's go inside and dry off now. I'll plan another picnic for the next rainy day."

Nature's Effect On My Day

Don O'Neal

During my aunt's final years in a nursing home, about once a week I'd pick her up and take her for a drive. First, we'd stop by Taco Bell and pick up some nachos and cheese, then drive down country roads and talk.

On this particular day, I remarked that the corn fields seemed about ready to harvest, to which she responded that, at the nursing home, one of the ladies had commented that one of the things she missed was the sound of dry corn leaves rustling in the wind.

So, as we passed the next cornfield I pulled over, shut the engine off, and we listened to the wind in the corn. Although we had both grown up in rural areas, that was something neither of us had ever done. That conversation brought back other memories in sound, like fire crackers on the 4th of July, the sound of "Taps" echoing through a cemetery, June bugs hitting the screen and the one I still enjoy, the sound of the screen door slamming. To this day, we have a screen door on our porch and we always encourage the grandchildren to "let the screen door slam!"

Nature's Effect On My Day

Michael Nelson

Nature has a very strong effect on me, which affects my writing. Nature can put me at peace of mind where the blocks to creativity are removed. The forest speaks to me inviting me to join with the woods. The shape of a tree can stimulate some universal truth in my mind. The flow of a stream can generate thoughts to write about. The presence of a deer, bird, or some other animal can be worthy of writing about.

Visits to the woods can change my thinking. Quite often the forest will make me write poetry or Haikus. The flow of thoughts can come fast so I jot down titles and notes to stimulate my writing. I may record thoughts on my phone, anything to jog my memory is helpful. Someday I hope to sit in the woods to write once my dog becomes calmer, I look forward to that day.

Nature's Effect On My Day

Eva Hahn

I am a weather watcher and weather warrior. I check the weather channel to see what they say is coming. If it is going to be very hot I am up early and outside before the day heats up. Only going in for breakfast when the heat becomes too oppressive. Then I shower and do dishes when I can't work outside. Then later in the cool, shady afternoon, back out to finish the job.

I love the gentle summer rains; they make me feel like a child. I often go out in my nightgown and walk through the gardens and pull a stubborn weed that now comes out of the wet ground easily. It is like cleaning up my life. I come in soaking wet and happy physically and spiritually clean.

Nature's Effect On My Day

Teri Freesmeyer

The breeze gently blows through the limbs as the leaves begin to shimmy and dance. The Air whispers her gift against my skin and massage the tendrils of hair in her soft words. The warmth of the sun tingles the bare spots of flesh and offers sustenance to the intricate parts of my eyes. Deep inside the brightness of the day has lifted the sleepiness and haze. My creativity is ignited as a spark of possibility arises.

A slow transformation occurs as I hear the distant rumble of hungry, thundering clouds gearing to burst. The thunder speaks to my heartbeat and excitement fills my spirit as the sky becomes magnetized as it offers the puffy chrysalis to shed its tears of joy and water the flowers. The exchange is soft, the droopy petals awaken and smile back at the rainbow. Transformation is sometimes quick like this and fragrant with change in a short time. While others are stretched throughout seasons.

Leaves falling slowly. Hardly noticing at first the shade has been altered until suddenly the skeleton of Mrs. Tree lounges bare in the silhouette. All winter she looms. Quiet and naked. Still and unchanging. And yet deep within there is a wisdom which springs forward months later in bloom. Sometimes our nature is slow, deliberate, and subtle.

Then warmth of the sun awakens the sleepy haze and ignites a spark of new possibility.

Nature's Effect on my Day

Ruth Souther

Oh the heat! A blessing or a curse? In the spring, after a long cold winter, I pray for those hot days of summer to begin. When they start, and that's after a rainy month or a 'bonus' cold month, I am like a cat stretching out and basking in the sunlight. I rejoice in the waves of warm air and dance barefoot on the fresh new grass, so happy to have survived another winter.

But now. Oh, the heat! It's slowly melting me down into a puddle of sweat and confusion. The waves I see may just be my own delirium as I gasp for air that is not supercharged with molten lava. The green grass of spring is brown and dried up and crunchy under my not so bare feet. I drag myself from a car that hasn't even cooled down by the time I arrive at home and into the cool breeze of air conditioning. Then I notice even the air conditioner is struggling keep up and parts of my house are still too warm.

I can't sleep without a ceiling fan, a floor fan and a fan by my bedside blowing directly on my face. Can't stand the weight of a blanket or the cat's body heat as she tries to snuggle. And my husband? Forget it, stay on your side of the bed, please!

I'm now begging Mother Nature to bring that delicious cool Autumn wind to me. Bring on Winter! I'm ready for sweaters and jeans and boots instead of sticky tank tops and clinging shorts. I'm ready for the leaves to fall so I can see further in the distance. I'm even ready for the walnuts to drop, even though they threaten my life every time I walk outside

I know my energy will flow and creativity will rise and I will once again feel human once the cold air arrives

Nature's Effect on My Day

Nancy Hodge Long

Each morning I awake with a sense of awe and wonder. The morning offers a moment to step out of my house and welcome the day. Nature greets me through all my senses. First, I notice the quiet, and yet subtle sounds like birds chirping and leaves rustling. My eyes take in the sky, clouds and the last twinkle of the morning star. The landscape fills my vision with large trees and round bushes; tall and tiny flowers of all colors; the lush green grass of summer; and birds flitting through the air. My nose finds the crisp scent of morning or the musky smell of heavy humidity. Often the fragrance of the hibiscus or clematis wafts to my nostrils. My skin opens to so many sensations - the light breeze or coolness and the warmth of the rising sun. My bare feet touching the dew on the grass brings a strong connection to nature. I am alive and grounded, grateful and ready for another day of nature's mysterious unfolding.

What If I Let Go

What If I Let Go

Nancy Hodge Long

What if I let go, really let go of all the stories that bind me to my identity? I'm not sure where to start.

Almost twenty years ago, I completed my first Yoga teacher training at the Himalayan Institute in Honesdale, PA. It was ten intensive days of Yoga and pranayama sessions, philosophy and nutrition discussions, meditation and chanting. No caffeine or chocolate or sugar. Vegetarian diet, of course.

I was terrified I wouldn't be "good enough" to be certified. I studied the mound of texts required and attended all sessions. At first I thought the strict dietary requirements would be my undoing, but I let go and flowed with ease into nourishing my body, mind and spirit with all things Yoga. Each morning before sunrise I joined about a dozen others in the meditation room. Sitting in silence with others became my favorite time of the day. I found it easy to let go of many of my stories, but not all. At some point during the training I heard others talking about receiving a personal mantra from the spiritual head of the Himalayan Institute. I was fascinated...

I had experienced TM years before, but that mantra never stuck. I fell away from TM before even really trying. But this time I truly believed it was my time. I requested a meeting with Panditji. Each day for four or five consecutive days someone would say "Be ready. Panditji may see you today."

After so many times of nothing materializing, I let go of the idea I would have a chance to receive a personal mantra and I was okay, fine with that. Then the next morning one of the senior teachers said, "Today's the day."

These mantras are "secret" and lose their power if shared, so I won't do that. But I will say one word ~ surrender.

What If I Let Go

Teri Freesmeyer

What if I let go of what if 's and simply wondered or wandered as if I were God's light in every moment?

What if I let go of any insecurity or fear and had absolutely no qualms about anything at all ...ever?

What if I let go of being someone or somewhere or an intended outcome or any need for support or recognition or gratification?

What if I let go of letting go of expectations and actually had intentional expectations? How would that influence the outcomes and what if I could let go of the emotional baggage that surrounds said expectations and found everything fascinating and glorious?

What if I let go of the rules and the variable ideals and influences of society, age, body, money, work and a slew of other 3-dimensional realities and simply went naked through life?

Naked Hearted. Raw and open, and filled and flowing with love and compassion.

Naked minded. A blank slate to simple breathe in the sensory carnival that nature, people and the universe provides.

Naked bodied. Painted instead of clothed, draped in luscious fabrics of the most exquisite textures and let it flavor the day in color and flow or sheerness for a just a slight illusion of protection or fluffy, fuzzy and organic to spend the day as a bear or a tiger, hibernating or pouncing about.

Naked writer. Letting go of the outcome to be a specific genre or topic. Letting go of the number of pages or organization of material. Letting go of the need to write a book, a paper, a poem, a best seller, or even self- helpful item article or essay and simply wrote raw undefined words that were meaningful for me in that moment so I could let go of that moment and move into the next caliber of letting go like letting go of the deranged and misarranged fossil of words on this topic

What if I let go and let everything be fascinating and glorious? Including me.

10 Minute Writing Prompt

Divine Intervention

Tim Crawford

Adam:

It wasn't until she got close enough for me to read her name tag that I got the joke. She had entered the far side of the conference room and was creating a wave of infectious joy as she hugged, air-kissed, aggressively high-fived, and explosively fist-bumped her way through the crowd. I couldn't, at first, make out what she was repeating, to uproarious effect, at each fresh encounter. Then, after she deftly executed a quick dance step with a giddy couple, I could hear that she was saying: "intervention, bam!" Her impromptu sprinkling of glitter on the bald head of a tall fellow, who accommodatingly stooped to accept the anointment after she inquired, "intervention?," was punctuated with a spirited "bam!" More glitter and more laughter in burst mode filled the air. "Intervention, bam!" I had to laugh when I saw it. Her name tag said "Divine." Her trajectory had her on a collision course with me. Yeah, that's how we met. It changed my life.

What Does It Mean When I Say Love

Teri Freesmeyer

What does it mean when I say "love"? When I say love, the duality of the fickle heart, my fears of humanity and the cracks from previous experiences shiver in contrast to the desire to love and be loved. The longing for closeness and companionship to the effervescence of infatuation of the new.

Oh, precious soul what does it mean when I say love? It means the freedom to be yourself as you discover, reclaim and get messy. It means the breath that fills your inspiration. It means the birds that sing you lullabies.

When I say love, I say it with waves and thunderstorms and tear drops of truth that bubble up inside when your heart beats in unison with your soul. I say love in changing seasons so each part of rest and growth has its moment. I say love through variety in color, shape, size and aroma.

To you my precious ones I say love in choice. Each tempo

and voice a place in the world and my love has no conditions or limitation. I offer you stars for gazing and moons to honor your phases and contrast and conflict and perseverance.

Love is not in the eye of the beholder. The eye, the beholder, and the space between is the love. It is the fiery sun and the transformative flame and in everyday miracles and yes even in the shame. I hold, I wrap you as the story unfolds. I offer you true love as from heaven to earth, from birth to death, from shame to compassion. I hold it all to my bosom. Precious One, you are my love. Created from love. Always held in love.

What does it mean when I say love? It means nothing and everything.

Yet you tend to believe your own definition. I love that. I love you.

Transcendent love, let me in. I call to you yet don't fully know your language. Or perhaps, remember?

Born of the Same Breath

Nancy Hodge Long

We are born of the same breath. The exchange of inhale and exhale connects us to this world. Scientists and mystics alike tell us we breathe each other as molecules and atoms float through the air moving to all corners of the earth. We join with all living things through the breath.

We enter this life with an inhalation and exit with one final exhale. With the inhale we open and draw in vibrant energy and all of life. As we exhale, we share what we have experienced. Exchanging with all beings this precious breath. How could it be otherwise than to be born of the same breath?

What My Writing Can Do For Others

Nancy Hodge Long

Often, I wonder if my writing has any purpose or value other than to offer a means of self-expression. I mean really what do I have to offer anyone? I barely hold myself together.

But then a light breaks through and shines so brightly that I can no longer deny my birth right as a human being. I know in a way that is deep and palpable. I am here to share who I am with each one I meet. Whether in a casual or deep relationship ~ each of us is here on this physical plane, in this body, in this time period for reasons we may never fully understand. In past encounters I have had students I don't recognize tell me how my one Yoga class years before changed them in ways that continue to impact them.

I struggle with my writing and my self-worth. But I recognize this is part of my path. It makes me human and enables me to truly feel what others experience, too. I know I am not this body, this mind, this persona. Who I am is so much more. Yet I express myself through these things. It is important to remember and not be attached.

Many years ago a teacher told me there are three things to living a successful, fulfilling life once you know your purpose. First, show up. Second, to do the work with a grateful heart. Third, let go of all control of the results. What a gift that was!

I sometimes forget, but when I don't, I know I am writing or speaking or teaching to offer a space for others to recognize who they are.

This is what I can do for others and it doesn't have to be laborious or overwhelming or beyond my ability. I just need to:

Show up

Write with a grateful heart Let go.

Doing Work With A Grateful Heart

Nancy Hodge Long

Life offers endless opportunities to be grateful. Sometimes it is only after being ungrateful that gratitude begins to blossom. Throughout my life "work" has taken different forms.

As a child my work consisted of chores like washing dishes or weeding the vegetable garden. Even as a 10-year old I recall the difference between doing work with a grateful heart or not. If I was upset with my sister because she reached the sink first and claimed "washing the dishes" as her work, I could spend the entire experience of "drying the dishes" as just horrible and unfair. Other times I remember thoughtfully, gently drying each plate, fork or spoon and actually enjoying it.

The same could be said of time I worked at the university library or as a waitress. All the years of teaching elementary school were daily reminders to "do work with a grateful heart." Although many days were difficult and gratitude was nowhere to be found, eventually I found myself back in the loving arms of gratitude.

Now as an adult, when I step into the Yoga studio, such gratitude fills my heart. I love every moment of my "work." Do others sense and feel this? I'd like to believe it radiates out and opens a space in each of them for gratitude to bloom.

Jar of Buttons

Nancy Hodge Long

When I was born we lived with my father's mother in a large house by the lake. Grandpa had died a few years before while Dad was stationed in Europe during WWII. After my grandfather passed away, my mother, newlywed, moved in with Grandma. The house had plenty of space and I particularly remember two spaces.

One was the front porch where Grandma kept her Singer sewing machine, the old foot pedal kind. I loved watching her as she stitched quilts and dresses, aprons and jackets. The smooth rhythm of her foot moving the machine along was soothing and almost mystical.

The machine sat in a wooden stand with two deep narrow drawers. Inside one drawer were all the loose buttons. Like a treasure chest, my sister and I would rout through the mounds of buttons searching for gems and precious jewels. We loved the bright colored ones, the pearls and especially the rhinestone buttons.

We'd ask Grandma if we could have the few chosen buttons of the day. Sometimes she said, "No, those buttons have a special purpose. I need them."

But many times she would smile and say, "Yes, you can have them. But don't put them in your mouth."

We would trade them or sometimes take the stones out and pretend they were rare jewels. Grandma would help us make little pouches with drawstrings to keep our treasures safe. I haven't thought of that house or those buttons for many, many years. But just listening to everyone and having "buttons" as a prompt have brought back precious memories of a time long past.

Enthusiasm

Nancy Hodge Long

Lately my enthusiasm has been lost. Somewhere along the way the fuel emptied from my engine and I've been stuck. It's hard to do much of anything without enthusiasm. Like moving through gooey molasses, all my energy is devoted to simply putting one foot in front of the other.

Oh, there are times quite frequently I feel a spark of happiness, contentment or even creativity. But it does not last. When I attempt to really act on it and accomplish something, the enthusiasm has dissolved. What to do? What to do? Come to writers' and receive that wonderful transfusion of enthusiasm from my favorite group of sister writers. That mysterious transmission of creative energy ~ enthusiasm!

Hide The Body

Nancy Hodge Long

Sigh ~ deep sigh... What are you ladies doing to me? Hide the body! I feel like I've been hiding the body for most of my life.

When I was young and asked questions like, "Where do you think we go after we die?" My mother would ignore me and my grandmother would launch into a discussion on the merits of living a righteous life so that you go to heaven.

Neither was satisfactory. I learned to quit asking after so many times of receiving blank stares or pat answers from Sunday school teachers when I was very young and professors while in college. Eventually I found a hidden body of knowledge that captured my attention and started me on a life long path. This esoteric body of ancient wisdom told me how we have more than a physical body ~ five bodies in yoga philosophy. And at the very center, our core body is Bliss. Now that's heaven!

So as I sat on my floor last week in total meltdown, tears flowing from deep hidden recesses of my bodies, I remembered. There is a hidden body and it is who I am. It is bliss and it is eternal.

How much will this help me as I move through daily challenges? Who knows, but I like having the reminder...

This Is What I Have To Say

Nancy Hodge Long

I'm foggy this morning. My eyes aren't focusing as clearly as I'd like and my mind is fuzzy. Some days are like that. I thought I was fine when I woke up, but now I wonder if I might need more than coffee.

How can things change so quickly I was in my car driving here, looking forward to a productive day? Then one text changed everything. I'm frazzled and helpless.

It's so strange watching how my emotions can be pulled instantly into dramas I have no control over. It is weird to feel my heart pounding and my mind ruminating. Then comes the judgment, the questioning. "Am I too selfish? Why not drop everything and drive all day to save him?"

No, it's not selfish to let him figure things out on his own. He has his path and I do believe he chose it, just as I have chosen mine. So, I guess I simply need to say, "Everything is okay, even though it is so very hard."

It's OK to Lie when...

Nancy Hodge Long

Here's what I have to say about this. A huge part of me says loud and clear that it is not OK to lie ~ ever. But the reality is that I lie or withhold my true feelings or opinion so often, I could probably be convicted of lying every day of my life.

For instance, my son called and said, "Mom, could you find a dentist for me and make an appointment? I'll be in Springfield August 20-22."

I wanted to say, "Look Jess, you need you do this yourself. You are almost 26. Time to take responsibility for your health."

Instead I said, "I will try, but you don't have insurance. I think there are low-income dentists. What's happening?" I immediately took the hook and enmeshed myself in the drama of his tooth pain and dental hygiene or lack of it.

I frequently keep my mouth shut when I have an opinion or say something just to please the person in front of me. I think the real problem is lying to myself.

Why Go to a Retreat

Nancy Hodge Long

Retreat – to back away from – to remove myself from daily routines and responsibilities – to nourish and rejuvenate.

What comes to mind when I consider attending a retreat? First there is time completely removed from my ordinary life. Although retreats may be just a few hours, I like the idea that they offer time to disconnect from my normal commitments. A retreat creates space of limitless possibilities for experiencing and expressing myself.

There is also an element of being an intimate part of a group of like- minded souls. Often being in the presence of others opens a space for creativity and transformation. We connect in unique and surprising ways, able to offer our gifts to each other. There is almost a magic to what can unfold when we are together in retreat.

Planting Seeds

Nancy Hodge Long

What can we call ourselves? As a group we are so diverse, eclectic, vibrant, and longing to make a difference. Now is a time to reassess who we are and where we are going. It seems we have a strong pull to create a book or maybe three, as a collective.

I like collective. It describes us giving us uniqueness, yet our commonality. Conscious is a strong word for the group as well as for writers of course.

Conscious Writers Collective (CWC)

We seem to be fumbling through a huge birth canal but rather than being alone in this birthing we are holding hands. Together creating something larger than each of us. Something we shall cherish.

From Overwhelm to Action

Nancy Hodge Long

The last so many days I woke up in overwhelm. For some reason everything feels like it's closing in. I take a deep breath and sigh it out. Returning to my center, I know everything is unfolding as it should. I just want to sense I am moving forward. I want to feel I will actually finish the project without losing my mind. After sitting in the quiet morning for even a few minutes, my confidence returns and I move forward into my day.

But lately it's one step forward and two or three back. I can't move into action when so many emotional ties and responsibilities are calling me to step into other worlds. So many emotions shouting to pay attention to everything except my project.

I am frustrated, discouraged and so very alone. Yet I know I have support from so many. Mike, the ladies of writers group and many students and others who causally ask, how's the book coming. I find it so strange to be in a place where I bounce back and forth between these two mental/emotional states. I haven't found the way yet to turn overwhelm into sustained action. But I am not giving up.

Moments of Messiness

Nancy Hodge Long

I'm wondering if messiness is okay. I mean really okay. Though deeply ingrained beliefs about being neat, tidy, and organized are strongly rooted in my psyche, I now wonder if this actually equates to general awesomeness.

I grew up with a mother who was highly organized and a grandmother who was neat and tidy to a "T." I tried unsuccessfully to carry on those traditions as I raised my children. Often my frustration to keep things in order was a sign that what I really wanted was to be with my kids and enjoy those moments.

Now I find my desk covered in piles of draft versions of my writing, random scraps of paper with important reminders, and various books I need to have close as I work. My moments of messiness tell me, I'm productive, maybe even creative. They remind me that creating anything is messy business.

Later I take time to sort, organize and clean my desk. Maybe I even delete old files from my computer. That feels so good, too. Taking a moment to see everything in its place.

Pause – take a breath- enjoy the moment. Then prepare for more moments of messiness. It's okay, better than okay, it's magic.

Poems

Teri Freesmeyer

I AM NOT AFRAID

I am not afraid of the gifts of my true heart.
To be an individual, to be a collective, a
community, a multi-dimensionality personality.

There is nothing wrong with me.
Bold and explosive, gentle and vulnerable. Filled
with electric pulses of song and dance.
Filled with tears of lost romance.
I am no longer afraid of the gifts of my wild and sensitive heart.

Juicy and deliberate with passion and pleasure.
Open and unobtrusive at times when observations are a treasure.
Cold and hidden when space needs measured.
I am not afraid of my shadowy depths, too deep for some.
I am not afraid of my shallow pools, too simple for some.

Fiery and impulsive ignited in creative orgasm.
Still unfolding defense strategies held in chaotic spasm.
No longer afraid to shed a tear or tear down the status quo.
I am not afraid to go inside the well,
the underworld, the alternate
realms
and retrieve yet another piece of my soul.

There is nothing wrong with me.
I am willing to embrace my lost and forgotten,
my long ago misplaced.
Willing to shine a light or be the light for myself and others.
I will also be the trigger. Sometimes the bullet.
Sometimes the lighthouse.
I am no longer afraid of the gifts of my true heart.
I am no longer afraid of yours.

Colorful or naked, I am the artist of my soul. I
can be a work in progress and still be a leader.
I can be the student and still the teacher.

The star of the show, the co-star,
the back stage hand or manager,
and even the audience.
I am not afraid to do the dirty, gritty, dark
and glittery work of being the
usher of new world energy. This is me.

I can digest it all and crawl into the comforts of my
earth cocoon, melt and die and fly. Freedom is my ally.
Girly, Goddess, Female, BadAssery Mastery.
Tomboy, Biker Chick, Belly Dancer, Lover and Loner.
Aunt who births none, yet mother to many.

I am not afraid to see the world through rose colored glasses.
Roses come in many shades as does the world.
I am no longer afraid to remember
how loved I am or I was or will
always be.
I am even learning to receive your love
as I learn to receive my own.
I am remembering I am love and that
I haven't loved or lived near
wild enough
from the fears I have had of loving and living.
I am no longer afraid of the gifts of my true heart.
I am not afraid to remember I am
wounded and lost, abandoned and
brilliant.
I am you. And I am not you. HA! I am not even me.
I am the priestess, the fool, the playmate. I am shocking and
strong. I am a Sacred Warrior. I am an Avatar of the Heart.
I am Shakti. I am
Sublime.
I am The Artist of my Soul, a work in progress There is nothing
wrong with me.
I am learning to decorate my imperfections with love,
I am not afraid to be the Hermit AND I am not afraid to be The
Moon.
I am not afraid to be The Sun or stardust or fairy dust.
I am not afraid to be human.
Today, I am not afraid.

Writing is Our Super Power

KALI CALLS ME TO THE FIRE

She calls me into and up from
She urges, she lures
The cycles of change, "endure, endure".

The Black Hole, the edge
The underworld current of chaos
Lost! Lost! Lost! Come on in and find me again.

Let go she calls, she beckons with fire and hope.
The fears, the poisons, let go up in smoke.

Dwell and stumble. Scream and fight, Your
will to struggle, your need to survive.

Survive the chaos or die to rebirth
Lies and deceptions have stripped your worth.

You're holding your own killers
You're suffocating the Earth
She calls with her flames. Let go for rebirth.

It hurts, it torments, it burns, it locks up
Until you step into the fires of love.

Sacred and warm. Dancing with lust
Flames of desire to help you combust.

She calls, she urges
Her power resides
It is there in the depths
Just come on inside.

Wandering the ashes
Disoriented by smoke.
The Ego disintegrates, no name to be spoke.

The beaker of healing steals thru your life
Sorrow and joy taste the same deep inside

Let go she calls, let me guide you through Relax
on the sidelines with nothing to prove.

Enter she smoothes with her bellowing grace

Into the tomb of Great Mothers gentle embrace
"heal my darling, heal you I will".
A partnership is needed for our world to be clear.
Love the delicate juices you've have bled.
Love the confusion from your lips you have said.

Let go and dive into the succulent web Take
charge and surrender this true you instead.

The fiery gates hold us down The watery depths sink your heart
Sacred Mother will hold you, till you choose to part.

She calls, she beckons me, into and up from
The cycles of nature with nowhere to run.

She urges, she lures "endure, endure".
Spirit whispers, spirit remembers "endure, endure".
The birth of Dragonheart is sure, is sure.

RISING FROM THE DEPTHS

Find me a place, be it planet or star
A ripening womb to burst forth from afar.
Ascend or descend, which way I don't know
So much to experience so many places to go.

Emerge from the depths, she whispers with tempt
Come swim in my waters or fly by nonexempt.
Handle with care or shine bright if you dare
Swirling and splashing, gasping for air.

Odd form arises, judgment stunts her growth.
She is determined and patient, honoring her oath.
There is light even faint, there comes encouragement ablaze.
Which world she chooses, which element displays.

Understanding flows yet is sure out of view.
Earth or spirit, star or water, how do you choose?
Whether in the depths of the ocean or depth in the skies,
Is the heart of all that is, be it vague or inside

Handsome and washed free, if only a short time
Merging Heaven on Earth is generously sublime.
Emerge from the Unconscious Goddess of Depths
Shine in Your whimsy, through life and through death.

Nancy Hodge Long

Poems from the Heart

When Grace enters life, there is a certainty and letting go of perfection. Life takes on a gentle flow, even when challenges emerge. Poetry can be a guide to right action or awaken a new perspective. The following offering is my personal journey inward, an anxious quest to know "who I am." The gifts of gratitude and the kindness of others have opened the path allowing Grace to lead the way.

Nature's Meditation

Green grass
Smooth stones
Gently flowing stream
Whispering breeze
Footsteps softly slipping
Toward tranquility

Butterfly

Intricate, delicate, carefree
The butterfly floats through its short life basking in the light.
Having struggled in the darkness of that cocoon
Not knowing
Not knowing
Not knowing
What life might be

Sisters

I believe sisters are here to hold a mirror
for us to see ourselves
as we truly are.
At times,
we may forget our beauty,
our generosity,
our lovingness.

Sisters remind us we are perfect just as we are.
Sisters give us space
to accept what life has given,
perhaps to see it through different eyes.

Encouraged, supported, and loved,
we can face whatever challenge comes with
courage,
grace
authenticity.

Sometimes

Sometimes in the still darkness of the night
Such sweet comfort wraps around me.
In moments like that
It's real,
It's real,
It's real,
It's all I need.

Divine Light

A million bits of light
Tiny, sparkling, glittering in space
Perhaps each a being of light
There to guide and support
Stay vigilant, awake and aware
Tiny beings are everywhere!

Darkness

Sometimes the darkness is everywhere
It feels heavy, thick, hopeless
When grief is present it can even be difficult to breathe.

The heart hurts deeply as if it is literally breaking.
The people and activity around you
appear far away and unavailable.
Nothing seems to soothe or comfort.

Then perhaps a moment of recognition,
an understanding beyond the rational mind
leads you to a point of light.
The light holds you
in perfect stillness,
utter softness.

It is in moments like these you know beyond all logic,
that this spark of light is always present.
Somewhere beyond
All is well.

A Chance

Once in a while there is a moment
when a difference can be made
when insight opens the heart
when honesty is the only choice.

Then the heart awakens
and meets another
in peace, compassion, truth.

Perhaps

Old resentments, hurts,
and misunderstandings can dissolve.
It is then real connection
finds its way into
the moment.

Morning Light

Golden streaks
Shades of pink and blue
White streams
Fading night
New delights

Stars in the Night Sky

Clear warm night
Blanketed in a soft breeze
Velvet indigo sky
Stars sparkle and twinkle
Seeming to send messages to my heart.

Oh, those stars
So close I can almost touch them.
What are they saying?
Little bits of sparkle fill my body, every single cell.
What are the messages?

Exuberance

I have a tendency toward exuberance
Bursting with joy is my favorite expression of life
For some it brings smiles
Others deep sighs
If only it could be accepted and enjoyed like
Old Faithful!

Dropping into THE Heart

Oh my, what does that mean?
This is not the physical heart,
Or the heart that holds a lover.
This is THE Heart, a space so vast it is beyond all knowing.
It is the home of True Nature,
The part of me that is changeless, ageless, and formless.
How to find this elusive Heart?
Rest back into the space behind the sternum
Let the mind with all its busyness drop down Just
observe by listening, sensing and feeling.
If the first few times there is no recognition, continue to look.
One day THE Heart will welcome me back home.

Listening

To listen, to truly listen ought not your heart be open?
To listen, to truly listen ought not your mind be quiet?
To listen, to truly listen ought not old beliefs be suspended?

Usual patterns of reacting held back.
Taking time to be in each moment as it unfolds,
without ego intruding,
might, just might, offer space to listen,
to truly listen.

Each Moment

Each moment arrives fresh and untouched by the mind.
It unfolds simply and is here for our experience.
If we can just allow and receive whatever is present,
We will realize peace
We will know joy
We will understand
The miracle of just Being.

Rest

What a joy to rest!
The mind works so hard to make everything perfect.
The body pushes to be just right.
The heart longs to feel safe and loved.

Resting, taking time to slow down.
Find and feel the breath.
Knowing there is nothing to do,
Nowhere to go,
No one to be
What a joy to rest!

Mother

Who is this woman who birthed me?
She carried me inside her own body
Giving me a body, a life.

I am mystified, confused, unsure
of the many emotions
frantically racing through my body

I sense this bond, deep and ancient that ties us together.
I need to know
I need to know
Because now I am the mother and my daughter is slipping away.

Bodhi

What is this pure joy that surges through this dog form?
He loves running, jumping, growling, shaking.
His body twists and turns
rushing in all directions at once.
He delights in the snow,
nuzzling his face deep into the white drifts.
He tries to catch and eat each snowball
we teasingly throw his way.
Once his energy is spent
he gladly returns to his bed for another nap.

Internal Stillness

I love to sit in the quiet of the morning
and feel the sensations of just being alive.
Life moves in predictable ways coaxing me
to leave this place of deep peace.
This internal stillness
is the most precious gift I have ever received,
I hold it in my heart
and seek ways to help it grow.
To be in this silence, this quiet, this stillness
and yet fully participate in each moment,
this is my deepest heart's desire.

That Moment of Waking

Upon waking,
my hand resting on my heart
reminding me,
This is where I want to be.

This place is not a structure,
yet it is my home.
Not the physical heart, the dynamic muscle continuously
beating and circulating blood throughout my body.

No, this heart space where my hand rests is
The Heart.
It expands and contracts with the breath.
No boundaries,
and yet some kind of barrier allows judgment and self-criticism
to dissolve when they reach this Heart.

Each morning,
this most precious time of the day,
I rest in the Heart
doing nothing
steeping in Gratitude

This Summer Morn

The sun is warm across my face as I open to another day.
The night has gone, its dreams barely a wisp of memory.
Where do I go at night?
It feels far away and without a body
There is always something happening
So real and alive
Yet upon waking, I know it was "just a dream."

Is it merely part of growing old
that the veil between awake and asleep has become so thin?
I'm curious, as I have always been,
What is life?
Why am I here?
How many more mornings do I have?
Will I complete my task?

Sometimes I wonder

Sometimes I lie awake
wondering When will it come, my
last breath?
Will I know it's coming?
Will I be afraid or simply curious?
Will there be time to kiss loved ones
and comfort them?

Life feels different now
knowing one day
I will drop
this body like a tattered jacket.

Kindness

Kindness is what we need
For ourselves and others.
If we cannot be kind to ourselves
Kindness will not be available to extend to others.

When the heart is closed
Kindness cannot reveal itself.
It is always with us,
We only need to keep our hearts open for it to emerge.

Waiting

I feel the pen wanting to move across the page
But it is not time
I sense my body wiggling, cells dancing under my skin
But it's not time.

Waiting
I acknowledge my mind racing, filled with words
But it's not time.

Waiting
Not knowing, yet knowing
I will wait until the moment arrives.

Megan McGee

Night and Day

The difference between the two is night and day.
Instead of fighting, discussion
Instead of mocking, compassion
Instead of slamming doors, communication
The difference is night and day

No more walking on eggshells
No more stress
No more threats
No more broken dishes
No more holes in the wall
No more broken heart
The difference is night and day

Where a slapping hand is now a gentle touch
Where a snarl is now a smile and laughter
Where anger and hatred is now love and compassion
Where distrust and accusations is now trusting and believing
Where "I own you!" is now "I love you!"
The difference is night and day

Just as the night turns to day,
my darkness is now brightened with
Love and compassion

The Good Wife

She was a good wife,
She did what she could to make him happy.
But dishes were broken,
Holes were punched in the walls.
But things will get better
Because she was a good wife.

He mocked her and called her "princess"
Said she was being femnazi
When she protested being treated as a servant.
She did everything to make him happy
Because she was a good wife.

He was hungry or just waking up,
So he couldn't be responsible for what he did.
He was forgiven for pushing her,
or holding her down, or hitting her
with the remote.
She cooked him lunch to make him happy again.
She should do what he said,
Because she was a good wife.

He worked a lot and was stressed so she took care of
everything, She cleaned and did dishes all herself,
Because she was a good wife.

Maybe if she did everything to relieve the stress,
Maybe things will get better
Because she was a good wife.

She kept guns and alcohol out of the house
Out of fear they would be used against her,
Because she loved him
And she was a good wife.

That didn't save her.
He woke up hungry and stressed.
He picked a fight, screaming and yelling.
She couldn't cook fast enough
Words were said, and she had enough.
As she gathered clothes, he started to shove her.

He shoved her onto the bed
Held her down to where she couldn't breathe.
As the darkness came, she couldn't help but wonder,
"Wasn't I a good enough wife?"

The Phoenix

From the ashes of a broken woman I rose
To live life anew

From the ashes of shy and self-doubt
To outgoing and confident

From the ashes of misery and anguish
To joy and contentment

From the ashes of broken dreams
To dreams realized

From the ashes of a broken woman I rose
Whole and complete

As a phoenix rising from the ashes
I start my life anew

I spread my wings of flame and soar away
from the ashes of a former life
And into a new and better one.

Jean Ferratier

Be Gone

The demon has been exorcised;
I didn't know he had been a tenant.
He had not the right to reside within me.
I had not posted a vacancy sign.
I thought he would have dissolved
Once exposed to Light but he was
Too Dense.
I banished him to take residency
At a new address;
The fiery gates of hell.
Not finding a working escalator,
He stepped into quicksand.

I watched with detached interest as
He was swallowed into the Nether World.
"Be gone with you," I said.
I turned my head and walked away.

The Life Within Me

Moistness on my skin.
Scent of recent rainfall.
Droplets on leaves.
Birds twittering messages.
Drums quieting my heartache.
Flutes soothing my soul.
Thatched shelter of leaves.
Lush greenery surrounding home.
Tiny arms and legs thrashing.
Plaintive voice wailing.
Face scrunched in indignation.
Scooping the babe from the fauna,
Moments ago emerging into light.
"I am here little one."
Tiny rosebud mouth sucking at my breast.
Striding away from the village,
To our spot beneath the banyan tree.
My child; gifted from one above.
Soul of my Soul.
My body cradling hers.
Fingers curling around my thumb.
Sighing with contentment.
Dozing, remembering my swollen stomach,
Singing to the life within me.

The Roots of the Earth

I have seen you from afar. I have seen you up close.
I have caressed your leaves.
I have felt the bump-bump of your bark.
I've watched you sway and rustle your leaves,
And lightning strike your friends.
Your leaves float softly in the breeze
To their resting places upon the grasses.
I have sought coolness beneath your limbs;
Even passed pleasant moments in repose.
Not until today, have I lain
Beneath the canopy of your shelter.
Lying on my back, I grasp the enormity of your height A
nd the intricacies of your branches.
Your roots support the earth
And my back which upon I lay.
Your nourishment comes from a central source;
Thousands of leaves sustained in their season.
You each are of an individual personality and character.
You are alive and rooted in the earth.
You my dear trees are truly grounded.

Diana Thornley

Hallway of Messages

Hallway of messages
Corridor of reasons
Truth prevails
Darkness speaks
Strangers listen

Fountain of truth
Sands of time
Static glow
On a mission

Altered images
Trails of lights
Stones of silence
Birds in flight

Cherubs dance
Angels sing
On a broken branch
Your memory clings

Hollowed virtue
Steamy night
In mind and soul
You're mine tonight

Regret and haunting
Another time
Hearts in love
Yours and mine

Tattered history
Memories in vain
Separate directions
Spilling love like rain

I want you to know

I want you to know
The right way
Have you since renewed your vows?
Separate lust from inevitable passion
Desire instead of aggravated hunger
Maybe it's better the way we are
Let our minds make love in the back of the car
Precious moments wrapped for hours
Product of an ionic compound
'INVITATION TO HEAVEN'
An angel spreads her wings making peace offerings
Sink within me till we are free
Like a hot air brush shooting warm colors
Illustrated perversion align the bathroom stalls
Where secrets pull themselves out of the woodwork

Varicose Veins

Varicose Veins run silently
Like muted trains winding
Helplessly in crooked lanes like a webbed fountain
Of bleeding tears

Feeling minute as an army ant
I succumb to her trenches like dust in the wind

Sun warms the universe gives strength to make them grow
Bathing the harvest saturating them row by row
Sun warms the universe every living thing
Bringing and taking life; to it we will cling

A girl born without the curse of paying her monthly dues
Is blessed with fertilization and motherhood has not denied her

Luna McGee

Primal

Her eyes made of water, her body of stone provides. Of
every rock, desert, and salt a new light grows. Above the
clouds and then the trees. What rays of hope so longer waits.

Piper sing your tune to me as drums beat to the rhythm
of the first heart, of bone and marrow she lies in wake.

Odin let your ravens soar high overhead. Feel the ravens
whistle as they take flight, may Ymir be evermore present.
The gods awaken the animal as she slips into
dawn, bones cracking, muscles stretching, of
dust and dirt unite.

Osiris with your flesh bright green, bring earth alive let deserts
roar, the sounds of corn and grass coincide with the roaring waters
Aphrodite seems to tread. Oceans so blue, skies so bright, the
wandering stars grip the sky as the gods scatter amongst them.
The birth of the warriors great and small prevail.
With night of one and day of two, the world seems
to shatter at the call, the warrior within the beast
comes to life as the drums dance through the air.

Siren's song of the seas in the night call to her with a
melody so true they speak the name of the oceans. What fate
has brought this warrior home, she will own the night.

The fear singing to the wind, the mountains bow and the
giants rejoice. From their forever homes thunder dwells.
Below, the serpent's hiss angrily.

Yggdrasil tree of life your spirit hears her call. Of snake
tooth, eagle claw, a solid snare of grace may your roots stay.
Yggdrasil live amongst the clouds, frostbitten
leaves so high above life, let your leaves of the
forest live forever.

Writing is Our Super Power

Sekhmet warrior of destruction and chaos, your reign of fire shown, of tooth and claw, fist and fang, fierce and roaring goddess. Warrior of the gods, Ra so softly strung your fate. Of primal instinct Sekhmet dwells below the belly of Hathor. Sekhmet hear the call of Bast and calm your murderous woe. Blade and shield swords strike hard as red dyed rum pours into the river from sky. Of blood unkept and poisons sending rain of sweet sorrow.

Hecate of night and magic dog let your cauldron brew, your frog sits amongst the goddess moon. Of Crone and flesh, daughter of time, let waves of calm fill the air. Open your book of shadows hand woven by fate, may the sleeping black dog lie. Let rest the night of fertility swell above the night spells are cast. Hecate of snake, dog, and sacred frog of night, let your shadow begin a new dawn to a better tomorrow.

The warrior who carries her weight in gold rides through rivers of sand. To find where she ends and all begins of every secret kept. Of ancient tomb and standing stone, the serpents hear her call. The goddess of fate so proudly sewn, the warrior rages on!

John Malan

Hades & Persephone: A Love Story

Hades and his brothers overthrew Cronus,
their savage father who swallowed his children whole.
The three brothers agreed to divide the world up:
Zeus took the Sky,
Poseidon the Sea,
Hades the Underworld.

Hades was so well suited to his realm
that he rarely left. Every day the number
of his subjects grew, pouring into the Underworld
but never filling it up.
Souls too wounded to move
beyond their suffering.

He was a good king, respected if not loved
for his fairness and compassion.
If he did nothing to improve their lot,
neither did he harm them in any way.
He did what had to be done,
and thought himself complete.

He often walked the borders of his Kingdom,
just below the boundary to the Middle World.
Never thinking there was more,
never caring to go beyond,
even if just to feel the warmth,
of the sun and wind on his face.

One odd day he heard singing, which brought him
up into the world of light and life.
Blinking in the sun as Persephone's soft voice
woke the seeds in the warming Earth
and drew the tender shoots
out of the darkness into Spring.

He was surprised to find himself there.

She did not see him, but went about her work
in loving kindness, and
did not hear his startled breath,
Persephone, tender, beautiful,
pure and innocent. Not meant for him.

Hades the warrior, Hades the great, confident
King of the Underworld
was struck dumb, his eyes grown round.
His jaw dropped, frozen in abject wonder.
All he believed was solid in his world
crumbled in an instant.

He was left him with a terrible, aching void
where his heart had been. He could not move,
still less think of taking her in any way.
Looking at Persephone,
he saw all that he was not.
All that he never imagined he could be.

Now could never be complete without.
He turned and fled, silently and instantly.
She did not hear a thing.
Back down to his great throne he went,
staggering like a drunkard, a blind man,
a man whose soul has been uprooted.

He could not eat, and neither wine nor water
moistened the barren desert that laid now
where his heart had been.
All that he had done,
held his vast Kingdom with pride.
None of it mattered now.

It was an illusion, made possible by the ignorance
that had blinded him so thoroughly.
There was no sleep that night,
the halls rang with his agony.
He could not keep his thoughts
inside his head but argued with himself out loud.

How he could not, could never return to the Upper World.
And yet, how he must, must, must
see her again, no matter the cost.
He settled to return just one more time,
stepping softly into the world of light
and saw her at her work in the Garden of Being.

Again, she had no sense of his presence,
and went about her work with joy and grace,
each footstep bringing splendor
to a darkened Earth.
Dumbfounded, he stood in silent awe,
and stared at her with adoration.

In what remained of his heart, he knew
himself to be unworthy of her love.
He knew she was unattainable,
knew that all he was and all he had done
meant nothing, and that he was, in fact,
no less miserable than the souls he lived among.

In that moment, she felt his gaze upon her and looked up.
Her startled expression grew wary and as
their eyes met, Hades felt fear for the first time.
He who had faced the rage of Cronus
without flinching, panicked.
He could not bear what he knew was sure to happen.

Rejection, loathing, ridicule.
The flaying of his soul and exquisite torture of his
deep and hopeless shame. Old warriors were taught
to go into battle with compassion and respect.
He had none for himself.
There was nothing there to save him.

And then, Persephone smiled and held out her hand.
Hade's heart expanded so much
his lungs were crushed against his ribs.
He could not breathe, yet crushed though they were,
he made a gasp when she came to him
and held him in her tender embrace.

The formidable gates opened with a sigh as
together they entered the Underworld.
The moment they stepped through
her light spread to every corner,
every nook and cranny. As she touched each soul,
the eternal hopelessness vanished.

There are some who say that in
all the time Persephone spent with Hades,
before her broken-hearted mother called her back,
she ate only six pomegranate seeds.
In truth, with all the heightened sensibilities and
appetites of new love, they feasted continuously.

But knowing the pain her mother felt,
and the joy that sang in her and her lover's hearts,
she settled at last on returning
with the number of seeds
that would keep the world and all that she loved
in true and proper balance.

It is said when she returns to the light and
the work of bringing life back to the surface,
that she forgets who she is,
and all that has happened.
It isn't long before Hades too forgets,
and begins to wander his kingdom again.

He feels that emptiness, that deep and sad longing
For something lost, yet unknown
until the moment when a gentle voice singing
alls him to the surface.
He stands in mute adoration, heart expanding
until she feels his gaze and the world is right once more.

Fiction

Short Stories

A Clam for Maggie
By Ruth Souther

A CLAM FOR MAGGIE, By Ruth A. Souther This story is dedicated to my Mother, Margaret Tipsword, a breast cancer survivor. It was first published in May, 1986 in Our Family, a Canadian magazine.

Clear, spring-fed Michigan water rippled around Maggie's knees as she waded around the shoreline of Gilead Lake. She delighted in the feeling of mud oozing between her toes. It brought back memories of better summers. Summers when she had done exactly the same thing: wade the deceptive waters, searching below the surface for sharp rocks. Rocks that, year in and year out, multiplied. A never-ending source and, until this year, a never-ending irritation.

This summer, the routine brought satisfaction to Maggie. It was positive. The results could be seen immediately. She glanced up at the pile of wet rocks on the shore. One rusted beer can set on top, its jagged edges faintly resembling a crown.

"Ouch." Her bare toes stubbed against a hard object. Maggie squinted at the wavering bottom of the lake. Her face was hazy in a distorted watercolor. Smiling, Maggie murmured, "Here I am, knee deep in life. Shouldn't I feel something?"

She plunged her hand into the water, searching for the rock. A chilly tingle went up her numbed arm. Digging deeper into the muck, she felt a slick, moss-covered surface. Maggie leaned farther over, nearly dipping her chin in the lake. Small bubbles popped the surface as the mud finally released its hold on the rock. Triumphantly, she looked at her prize, streaming with cloudy water and gooey with muck.

With a small shiver of delight, Maggie realized it wasn't a rock. It was a granddaddy clam, and from its appearance, it must have been in the lake forever.

"Do clams live forever?" She jokingly addressed the shell. "Or does it just seem like forever?"

She swished the clam through the water to wash away the excess slime and examined it again. Dark and light rings on the shell surface showed its growth stages. How on earth had the thing managed to avoid the usual fate of lake clams? Most became fish bait long before gaining so many rings.

It was a rare creature to have reached old age.

Perhaps it was enchanted, Maggie mused. She rather liked the idea of finding an enchanted clam. It suited her mood. And what if she were to kiss it? Would it turn into a handsome prince with magical powers?

A sudden stab of pain caught Maggie unawares. She gasped and brought her free hand to her chest, touching the area where a breast had been. Tears stung her eyes, blurring the beloved landscape.

Magic. Magic existed in fairy tales. She gripped the clam tighter as she pressed her fingers into the deep ache in her chest. Grandmother always talked about the magic of Heaven, what a joyous moment when the horn of Gabriel blew! The only catch was you had to die to get there.

Well, Gilead Lake seemed like a little piece of Heaven. Maggie scanned the peaceful horizon and wondered how this place could stay the same year after year. Especially when the rest of her world had shifted and caved in.

A soft, hesitant cough intruded on her thoughts. An alien face peered at Maggie from the shore several feet away. Startled, she first thought the entire lake was a dream and she was still wrapped in gauzy confusion at the hospital. The foreignness of the features confused her. The woman standing on the weedy bank pointed at the clam in Maggie's hand and spoke with excitement. Only a smattering of broken English words was understandable.

Maggie stared at her. Who was this woman? Why in the world did she want the clam? And what was she doing here in the first place? Blinking, Maggie shook her head. She didn't understand.

The small Asian woman, dressed in a swimsuit and beach robe, smiled and pointed to herself. Carefully, she enunciated, "Mai-Ling".

She gestured toward the cabin next to Maggie's. The cabin belonged to a minister who was always lending it out to those in need of an inexpensive vacation. Mai-Ling began to speak again. She swung a pink plastic bucket hanging on her arm. A word that sounded vaguely like 'chowder' reached Maggie's ears.

The meaning dawned on Maggie. She clutched the clam to her aching chest. Shaking her head, she intended to leave no doubt in Mai-Ling's mind as to whom the clam belonged. A puzzled expression settled on Mai-Ling's face.

Maggie looked from the bucket to the clam in her hand. Should she be polite and give it up? Should she sacrifice her enchanted clam simply because this woman asked her to? Poor thing. A few minutes ago, it had been snug in its hideaway under the mud and now, it faced a cookpot.

"No." The shout burst from her lips. She was shocked at her own vehemence. After all, the clam was a simple creature born only to turn around and die.

Blow, Gabriel, another of God's creatures is ready to bite the dust, is that it? Maggie held the clam aloft for a moment. Give it up, because death is inevitable? She hesitated for a second before hurling the clam far out into the mucky water. The sudden jerk of stiff muscles brought excruciating pain. Tears streamed down her cheeks. Once the tears started, they couldn't be stopped. Maggie brushed her fingertips across her face, leaving a muddy streak across her nose.

Embarrassed by Mai-Ling's steady gaze, Maggie felt her way along the rickety dock beside her. The rough, splintery wood felt good. It seemed normal the way picking up rocks was an every-year occurrence at Gilead. Maggie hoped she would prick her finger with a piece of the weather- beaten two-by-four and bleed. Yes, bleed. And bleed. And bleed. Blood meant life.

The overwhelming rage inside her centered on the small creature and on the unknown visitor. Six months ago, Maggie had been like the clam. Buried in her own small-town hideaway. And cancer had come visiting in the guise of a lump in her breast. The cancer had uprooted her life. It had sucked the soft inner soul from her body and left an empty shell.

A shudder raced down Maggie's spine at the gentle touch on her shoulder. She flinched, drawing away. She could not apologize. She would not apologize. The touch strengthened. With reluctance, Maggie turned to meet the other woman's gaze. Mai-Ling's eyes held concern and quiet sympathy.

'Pity. She feels sorry for me.' Panicking, Maggie touched her caved chest. 'And she knows. She knows about the cancer.'

Fighting the absurd inclination to laugh, Maggie saw herself through the other woman's eyes. Crazy American lady. Throw away perfectly good food. Sentimental over an unfeeling, cold-blooded creature. Ridiculous Americans.

Mai-Ling took her hand from Maggie's shoulder, reached into the pink bucket, pulled out a green-tinged clam and pressed it into Maggie's clenched fists. With difficulty, Maggie relaxed her fingers to take it. She stared without comprehension at the clam. What was she supposed to do with it? She raised her head and met Mai-Ling's steady gaze. Dropping her chin, she once again stared at the smooth, hard shell in her hands. This one wasn't as big as the first one. It had tiny nicks along the edge with the two sides joined, as if something had tried to pry it open.

Smiling shyly, Mai-Ling touched the shell with her finger and nodded toward the center of the lake. She made a throwing gesture. Maggie ducked her head as a new batch of tears filled her eyes. She wiped the back of her hand across her nose, smearing the streak of mud. Gaze blurred, she stared out at the peaceful lake.

With small sounds in her throat, Mai-Ling urged Maggie to throw the clam after the other one. If Mai-Ling could speak English, Maggie wondered if she would say, 'You silly woman. You wanted the clam and now I have made a gift of it to you. Why do sit there and stare at me as if I were the crazy one?'

It suddenly became of the utmost importance to return the second clam to the lake. Maggie gauged the distance and tried to put the shell in the exact same spot. With any luck, it would land nearby. The two women watched the graceful arc of the shell and heard the plop as it broke the surface and sank beneath the waves.

Mai-Ling waited for the last ripple to fade away before she pulled another clam from the bucket. This time Maggie did not hesitate. She flung the creature as hard as she could toward the center of the lake. The pain in her chest felt good.

Three more times, Mai-Ling reached in the bucket. Three more times clams found their way back to their neighborhood. Maggie's spirits rose as each one settled out of sight.

One more clam lay nestled between the upturned palms of the woman beside her. Maggie paused and searched Mai-Ling's shining eyes.

"You," Maggie cried, "You throw it."

Mai-Ling nodded. She hefted the clam as if weighing out life itself. As the clam sailed from Mai-Ling's fingers, Maggie tilted back her head and laughed out loud. Maggie's shout of joy echoed across the water. It was answered by the screech of wheeling lake gulls. A fishing boat rocked as its curious owner peered toward shore. A dog barked and a child giggled. A hungry fish flopped in the air, snatching at a mayfly.

The lake fell out of suspension and came back into life.

In the many years since this story was written, my Mother and Mai- Ling became close friends, writing to each other, sharing life's joys and griefs. Mai-ling and her husband eventually returned to the United States and had a beautiful reunion with my parents. Sadly, both women have passed away, but I imagine them standing at some lake in their private Heaven, giggling and talking and perhaps even returning clams to their muddy spots under water.

Death's Midwife

By Ruth A. Souther

The old woman sat with her head forward, gaze adrift in the flowered print of her dress. Her white hair was short and thin, with patches of pink scalp showing through. Years of hard life had left her fingers twisted and ankles too swollen to carry her more than a few steps away from her porch, yet she smiled to herself as she rocked. The bent cane chair creaked much like her bones, resisting the movement.

"Hello, Grandmother." A young woman stood with one foot on the first step of the rickety stairs, her left hand resting lightly on the iron railing.

The old one shook her head at the young girl standing before her. "I bet ye call all us elders Grandmother, don't ye Child?"

The old woman's laugh bubbled up in a deep rich sound denying the ninety-eight years of her life. "Though I don't mind, not a bit. Haven't heard it since all my children up and left." She nodded, lost for a moment in the past. "They was all good kids, too good fer here, I reckon."

"You have lived long and well, Grandmother, with many offspring, including both blood and soul family. It is my honor to be here."

"That's right kind of you." The old lady squinted, one hand lifted to shade her eyes though the porch was a cool oasis in the heat of the day. "But I don't recollect yer kinfolk. Who be you?"

The girl responded with a chuckle, hinting at a secret joke. "My name is Medea."

"Well, Medea, what is it ye want today?"

"I think you know already." Medea smiled, a sweet expression meant to comfort the old woman. "I have come to take you away from here."

"What if I says I don't want t' go anywheres? What if I want t' die here? Been here all my life, birthed my babies, raised 'em on up, found some more little ones that needed a home, buried a few, includin' my man. I don't really want to go anywheres."

"Ahh," sighed Madea as she sank down on the first stair. "I only want to do what is best for you."

"You don' know what's best for me, Child."

"I know you've lived a long life filled with a love so great it healed the hearts of many lost souls. You have shared your compassion with generations of children, when they had nowhere else to go. Your kindness is legendary, Grandmother. I am here to offer you the same respect." "Don' want it. I jus' did what I was supposed to do. Don't mean anything, really."

"It is time, though. Let me be as generous to you as you have to all those who went before." Medea played with the hem of her skirt, smoothing it across her knees before asking, "Aren't you curious to know where you're going?"

"They say curiosity killed the cat, and I ain't no cat." The old woman shook her head. "No sirree, I's happy here." Her gaze soared to the mountains in the distance. "I used ter run along the tops of those there hills."

"You will run again, Grandmother."

The girl spoke with a gentleness that made the old woman shed a tear. "Not in this here life," the old one wiped the drop away as her faded eyes wandered to the dusty path leading away from her house.

"No," the girl agreed. "Not in this life." Medea's fingers crept up to cover the age-spotted hand nearest her. "Truly, though, you must come with me. There is nothing left here for you."

"I ain't goin' without us having a chat first, Granddaughter." The old one focused on Medea's eyes and beamed a sly grin. "Been awhile since I had a chat."

Startled, the girl withdrew her grip. "Granddaughter? I have never been addressed in such a way." A smile lit her tender face. "I like it." She nodded, "Yes, I like it. Go ahead, then and let us talk."

Grandmother began to rock again. "Death, or leastwise one of his own, came to this stretch last week. Sure enough did, up and took Tillie's babe. Silvia tried to save him, lil' bit that he was, but he was snatched up with hardly a breath in between birthin' and dyin'."

Grandmother's head bobbed up and down as she gave a wheezing cough. "It was awful hard on Tillie bein' as it was her first. The babe was scarce a minute old with no chance of knowin' what he might'a been. It was real sad, it was. A mama's love sure devours the heart with pain when there ain't no babe to hold."

"Why so, Grandmother? Is death less appreciated than life? They are both gifts."

"Tillie's babe didn't have a chance to know life. Nuthin' to appreciate about that."

Unperturbed, the girl laced her fingers around one knee. "Is it not possible that desire might be better than breath?"

"Ye mean, what is at the end o' life? There's a question that ain't got no answer," Grandmother retorted. "Ye calls it 'desire', I calls it turrible. Death haunts us all 'r lives and in the end, he catches us, sure 'nough."

"But Death brings peace," protested Medea.

"So does life so why won't he leave us in peace until then?"

"Well..." the girl cleared her throat. "I don't know."

"He don't even come his self, but sends his creature..."

"Death's midwife is no creature." Medea's cheeks flushed. "Who do you think moves between here and the Shadowland where Death waits? The midwife guarantees safe passage."

"An' what of those left behind who weeps for the ones gone? She ain't got no feelin's for them? Kinda cold-hearted, ain't it? Don't show no caring, that's fer sure."

"What's left behind is not her concern." Medea straightened her shoulders and brushed off an imaginary bit of fluff. "She only cares for those who are leaving."

"That just ain't right." Grandmother shook one gnarled finger at the girl. "Why don't Death care? He gets us sooner or later."

The young woman shrugged. "Death is called, you know. He doesn't just...pick..."

"Called? Like on one them tellyphone things?"

"Not exactly like that, but still, called," Medea insisted.

"And Tillie's babe called out to Death?" The old one snorted. "Bein' just a few breaths with the world?"

"Of course." With one finger held up, she added, "I know you'll want to know why. Perhaps he didn't like what he saw. Maybe his reason for being here was already done."

"He was too young. Way too young. Not like me."

"Not like you," Granddaughter agreed. "No one is like you. No one knows like you."

"They says that Death is a han'some fella, and his midwife, well, she's a pretty little thing, full o' kindness for them that's dyin'." The timeworn granny winked, the creases in her face deepening. "But who'd really know, seein' as how she takes ye to the Shadowland and leaves ye there. Not much ye can say after that, is there?"

"I suppose not."

The two women sat in a companionable silence until the old one grunted and shifted in her seat, then spoke again. "How do ye know when ter call? How do ya know it's time?"

"You feel it." The girl brushed a silky strand of hair from her cheek. "Like the wind."

"How do ya call to sum'un like Death?" Grandmother whispered, a bit afraid. "I mean, when I'm ready."

Granddaughter rose to her feet. "You have already called."

"I su'pose I knew that." The old woman reached to take the young, strong hand held out to her. "I su'posed that was why ye was here. Didn't think it was just to pay a visit."

"But it's been nice…talking…" Death's Midwife smiled. "You truly do have a humble spirit, and that's not easy to find in this difficult world."

"Thank ye, granddaughter, fer all the day's I been here." Grandmother stood up, delightfully free of pain.

She felt feather-light and could breathe in the clear air without coughing. Eyes that had been clouded could see again. She danced a little jig before leaping to the ground, the story of her life bursting forth in a song.

"You're welcome," the young woman answered as she followed along behind. "You're welcome."

Excerpts from Larger Work

Excerpt from the Glass Cauldron Mystery series, book five, *Sacred Grove of the Galère*
By T. L. Woodliff

The Voynich Manuscript: A single book of high-quality vellum carbon-dated to the early 1400s. 20th Century code experts have failed to decode the material found within. It is now housed in a Yale library, an unsolved mystery that is missing several pages.

Malleus Maleficarum (The Hammer of Witches): Though written by a discredited clergyman in the late 1400s, this book was a bestseller, second only to the Christian Bible, for almost 200 years. It resulted in the torture and murder of thousands in the brutal search and prosecution of witches.

Tymph

Excerpt from the Glass Cauldron Mystery series, book five, *Sacred Grove of the Galère* by author T.L. Woodliff.

It was dark. Not dark as in *thunderstorms are sweeping across the night sky*. This was stuck-in-the-root-cellar dark; no chance of moonlight breaking overhead or the dim dance of far-away stars to twinkle away the stress of his Awakening.

This is wrong, Tymph thought. He held back the over-whelming urge of First Breath, his oak form switching to take in oxygen, now that he had lungs once more. *This is wrong.* He didn't know *how* he knew something was tainted this time. He had only vague images and emotions of being alive before now, no strong memories. But he knew it.

He knew it in that way you know killing is wicked, that the sun will rise to start each day, that the sound of laughter from children is a good sign the villagers aren't starving.

Light flickered inches away from his eyes. He gasped despite his resolve. He was a tree, after all, and fire in his face was to be avoided at all costs. So, he filled his new lungs, pretenses dropped.

"I thought so." It was the voice of a man, a young man, he judged.

Human. What was that language? *German?* Tymph's mind roiled as it tried to cement a place and time for this incarnation.

The light died as suddenly as it had appeared. His barely stifled a sound of appreciation. What could spark with such ready intensity? He heard the sound of shuffling feet against stone as the man moved away. *Injured? Am I here to heal?* The small thump of hands on wood told him the man leaned against a table. His breath sounded more than ragged- Tymph tasted his exhaustion as he inhaled. It surprised him to realize he could smell something like that. What else might he learn by scent, alone? Was the sense heightened, able to eek out mysteries never known because there was only a world of nothing for his eyes to discover?

A thousand questions formed but he pushed them away, not wanting to miss any clue.

Steps again. This time, they took the limping man upwards, above his head. Stairs. He was below ground, Tymph realized as a humidity settled over his leaves to confirm it. The water held the taste of soil and stone, compacted for ages with little life squirming through it.

Deep below the earth.

"I will return after I've rested." The man paused, snickering through his fatigue. "Get some rest yourself, daemon."

Why the laugh? Tymph waited until the sound of the little man's footsteps faded. He'd climbed a long way, he realized. The great tree stayed still for a time, stretching his senses to detect... anything. Some thought already nagged at him. What was it? Something strange, or rather, wrong. This manifestation was, even now, three-shades-of-shadow strange, and he'd been here mere minutes. He tried to sort through his jumbled memories, snatches of previous lifetimes spent in service to various witches and sorcerers.

He'd just been called a daemon, which he didn't appreciate. He was Silvis. Surely someone with enough power to call for his Awakening would know the difference? The limping fool knew enough to identify a marked oak and hide it down below the earth to call Tymph's spirit into it. How could he do that and think the Silvis had anything in common with daemons?

But that wasn't what nagged at him. It was something about the light. He still had no idea what the human had used to create instant flames, but it was more than just the sudden fire. What was off about-

Height! He almost shouted the word, but stopped himself and closed his mouth with a *chmp* sound. Before the man had pulled the light away, Tymph realized he'd been looking eye-to-eye with a human.

But that's not possible. Tymph always incarnated as an oak tree, tall and majestic. He knew he was one this time as well.

He craned his neck to look down. Only... he didn't. He tried again, wishing to see if his body was in a hole of sorts. But he couldn't move his head. Not that he would have seen anything- the darkness was whole. He tried to bring his branch-hands to his neck but found they wouldn't respond to his command.

Panic swept beneath bark as he struggled to move everything, *anything,* at once. Nothing worked beyond his eyes and lips; no branch would bend, no leaf pushed outward to explore what confined him. The darkness and the immobility were complete.

Tymph was trapped.

"BOVVER EYT," HE swore, using the slang of one of his previous masters. He'd enjoyed her company enough to take on a few of her strange, English phrases. He wished he could remember more.

Tymph mentally cringed and waited. Then he released a soft sigh. No winds had come to claim his words and tell the limping little speck of a human that he could speak. If Tymph had deduced correctly, the sorcerer didn't know his trap was incomplete. He would have asked him a question, or waited for a response when he spoke. But he neither tested his speech nor Tymph's ability to move.

He's very sure of himself. Tymph began to do what he'd always done- create a mental file, sorting the new master's character and traits, weaknesses and strengths into his branch-memories that would be easy and quick to recall through this entire lifetime.

The panic was gone. He'd never been in this particular state before, to be sure, but there had been more than one prickly patch to navigate, he knew. He rustled his leaves. Or rather, he *remembered* rustling his leaves, which was just as satisfactory. Or, almost.

Okay, it wasn't close, but it would do. Even waking up to find himself in a trap wasn't enough to dampen his spirits. He was alive again! The magic of the Earth-Mother and her mysterious need of the Silvis was alive, awake and ready to learn something new.

That was key, he realized with the keen insight of remembering what he already knew. Each lifetime provided an opportunity to learn something that would be important when it was needed. *Which is...*

whenever it's finally needed. He swallowed his own impatience with the Goddess of Earth for working in her slow, hard-to-understand ways. That was always his problem to work on, and maybe this new life, this *trap,* was to teach him patience.

Alright then. He allowed a brief smile, but hid it at once, just in case the little man had placed eyes in the darkness, so to speak. He was ready for the challenge. He would claim patience. He would master being idle and getting nothing done. Absolutely nothing. Nichts. Asgję. Res. Nihil.

Yes, this will be a short life, indeed.

Unfortunately, the great Silvis was all too correct.

TYMPH SOMEHOW MANAGED to keep his mouth closed as he jumped into another Awakening, and another trap. He smelled the exhaustion of the sorcerer, felt the dampness of his underground cell and knew himself to be in the same spot in which he'd died one year prior.

This isn't right. The panic was sharper this time, lasting more than seconds as it had before. Tymph knew where he was. He knew it because he *remembered* his last life with complete clarity. It didn't feel at all like an Awakening had occurred, just... just a waking up. And again, no light of the sun to greet him. No dance of the stars to mark the seasons. He was back here, back in this hole of want and a darkness so complete Tymph could almost believe he'd Awakened in the Ether between realms of life.

As though to argue his last thought, the flicker of a candle drew his eyes to the far corner. He still couldn't turn his head to see, but the peripheral vision of the Silvis is a notable gift. The same little man leaned over the same, wooden table, now moved to the side, taking deep breaths.

Good. Tymph was surprised at his own vindictiveness, but he was glad it had taken so much from the human to Awaken him this time. The idiot of a sorcerer had starved him to death, after all.

But how? How did he call me back?

This was a thing he'd never thought possible. *Such a thing!* Pulling a Silvis into an Awakening requires an enormous amount of energy. It's rare that a witch or sorcerer can manage it alone one time, much less twice, and with the same Silvis? Tymph would have said it impossible.

Yet, here he was. Again.

As the man rested, the great tree battled indecision. *Should I speak this time? What if the sorcerer starved me because he has no understanding of my requirements? I never spoke a word, even when the hunger was want to drive me mad. Was that wrong of me? Should I speak with him, tell him....*

Tell him how to keep me alive longer so he can continue to steal my earth energy. No.

A resignation settled over his form. He would not let the man know he could speak, nor that if given food and drink he would last for centuries.

"Let's try this again, daemon. I have your soul. You must obey me."

Must I? Tymph's lips burned to twist in a sneer. The man did not fully understand the situation, it seemed. Tymph's mind, and soul, was still his own to command. He stored the knowledge, keeping it close.

Something must have shown in his eyes, for the sorcerer bent forward, searching them. He pulled over a chair, nothing more than a stool to perch upon, and lit a lantern with three sides of mirror. This was more light than he'd spared the last time Tymph was here, combined. He returned the man's gaze, though his peripheral vision was seeking out every shadow and nook of the room.

"I know your gift, daemon. And I know your name. You cannot escape. Give in this time, and I will water your roots. I will provide nourishing soil that you might feed, and rest well. Do not fight me this time."

It took everything the great tree had learned to keep his eyes from showing emotion. He knew he gave away his thoughts with each expression- it was something he'd been working on for eons, literally.
He filed away the new knowledge: Confirmation the sorcerer doesn't know the Silvis eat and drink; a claim to know his unique gift and name; a belief the Silvis could provide a higher rate of transfer of the earth magic.

That last surprised the great tree. Had he somehow lessened the flow of magic from his body into the large crystal kept somewhere in the room? Tymph had never seen it, but he could certainly *feel* it. It was like a tube running from his veins to the stone, taking blood in a constant, draining pull. But it wasn't blood. It was everything that made him Silvis; it was Gaia's own magic.

And yet, the human expected it to be more. Could Tymph do something to slow the process? And what was its purpose? Witches and sorcerers Awakened a Silvis for power to *use,* not store.

He wanted answers to these questions. *But how? How do I communicate with...*

With only my eyes; my silly, expressive eyes.

Hmmm, but what character to gain the knowledge I need? What emotion must I draw from the sorcerer? Tymph had learned many lessons about gathering information. So much so, he was convinced that's why the Earth Mother offered him the fruit that took him from man to tree, many lifetimes back.

He chose a course of action and followed through. Tymph narrowed his eyes. Defiance. He would make the human think he'd held back the magic intentionally. He needed to know what this sorcerer had on his shelves of power that he might use against the Silvis to force a more powerful flow.

Some part of him shivered. He'd been misused more than once in his many lives. It wasn't something he usually sought. But if the sorcerer thought he could transfer more energy, then he had to know what the sorcerer knew. Tymph had to keep him on this focus. Patience was obviously not the lesson here. He visualized a loud snort that was almost satisfactory at the idea. *When you're wrong, Tymph, you are wrong.*

Now though, he had a solid, worthy lesson of a Silvis lifetime. The Earth Mother wouldn't waste one of his incarnations on something as simple as *patience.* He'd been a fool to think so, and had paid for it. Starving to death had not been a pleasurable experience.

He wished he could remove the branch of that memory. He'd just as soon never think of it again.

He was, however, doomed to repeat the experience.

THE DARKNESS LIVES. That's what the Earth Mother wants me to learn. Tymph's eyes rolled back in his head. He welcomed the approaching end to his constant misery. But the sorcerer pushed the acorn paste into his nostrils once more, the acidic tannins leaching into his system as soon as it touched him, forcing a lifeline of nutrients to keep him rooted in time.

Damn you. The tree wanted to scream the words. Perhaps the shock of it would cause a heart attack in the miserable, fool of a human. But he knew he could only manage a whisper, and things would become far worse. That in itself seemed impossible, but the Silvis knew it was true.

He would be kept alive, and Tymph refused to do anything that might support that outcome. This death had dragged on for months. *Hadn't it?* He had no light by which to judge time. No rhythm of bird flights to rejoice in the seasons. Only endless, constant, complete night.

And a hunger he never knew possible.

That unique pain was the discovery of a leviathan in the sacred stream. The invisible chains that kept him from seeing the sky was a misery almost too much to bear, yet the escape of a promised death kept him calm, accepting. But then after weeks, a panicked weakness poured over his existence and consumed him. His body, frozen though it was, spiked every nerve signal moving to his brain to *get moving and find food.* Even while he transformed into a living shade, the giant named hunger wouldn't let him rest. When the sorcerer was done with his experiments for the day, sleep was only a brief visitor. His body knew it might never awaken if he didn't first take nourishment. He begged the Goddess to release him with every ragged breath.

The sorcerer had failed to create a faster pull of power through his now stolen body. That's how it felt to Tymph- his body no longer belonged to him. He only had a brain, a brain that received signals of pain and need. The sorcerer controlled the rest. He broke branches and added them to his potions; collected Tymph's falling tears before they touched the stone floor; peeled his thickest bark to burn while chanting evil phrases in a language Tymph had never heard.

That scared him most. The Silvis incarnated all over the globe, knowing the languages of those around them as soon as they Awakened. Why did he not understand these words chanted over his burning body?

A shiver ran through his emaciated form. They were almost constant now. He rejoiced in each one as they had signaled the end of his last life. Surely this one was to end soon? What could the Earth Mother expect him to learn in this condition?

If the lesson is that darkness lives, I accept it, Great Mother! Let me die. Let me leave this place and enter one with the sky and earth restored.

He swallowed a great moan as the sorcerer ripped a small branch from his canopy. Fortunately, it held no memories. Or at least, he felt no loss, as was a normal feeling after such an attack.

A part of him whispered a desperate idea at that moment, one that made him shrink within himself.

The sorcerer had never asked for a branch. He either did not know this would create a great amount of magic- a Silvis giftbranch was as rare as a sighting of the Green Man and thus, powerful- or he thought Tymph would not give him one.

But what if he did? What if he offered him one in exchange for the gift of death? There was no possibility a sorcerer could pull a Silvis back a third time. The second spell had almost killed the little man.

Tymph would lose a memory, but he would leave behind this living hell. He would see the sky again. Or…. Or he would not. The Mother might keep him in eternal sleep for such a lapse. Could he live with that? Could he accept failure on such a level?

The great tree swallowed again and let the idea fade away. It was something about himself he would never know. Not because his strength of will was unstoppable. Not at all. It was because his logic would never accept the risk. He could not know if the sorcerer would live up to his end of the bargain. There was no way to assure it.

None.

And thus, he felt the thought drop away. It would do nothing to hold it another moment.

Above his head, a branch broke, seemingly on its own. The sorcerer's head snapped upright. Tymph, though, paid him no attention. The Mother had granted him a gift when he let the thought go. That tiny branch was all that was needed to send him over the edge, and into death. He would go where she would send him, but he would be himself, still Tymph. He would still hold to his truths: The sun will rise tomorrow; the singing of children tells us the village is well. Killing is most often a wicked thing.

But the sorcerer's voice followed him into the release. Before death claimed him, he heard the curse: "We'll do it your way, daemon Tym. A little at a time. I'll keep bringing you back until I have what I need. I'll be here, at the next Solstice, waiting for you. You are mine, daemon. Forever."

THE SCREAMS OF the female met him as he Awakened. *This is*

new, he thought with a numbness that brought him comfort in its familiarity. Hadn't he always been this way? The great sorcerer had awakened him....

He paused to think of the number, wanting to get it right. How many times had he returned to the dark world? It would help if the other Silvis wasn't screaming so loud.

Tymph tensed and opened his eyes to seek out her form. *We mustn't show the human that we have mouths!* He could no longer remember why that was important, but it was paramount to everything. He knew it. He knew it like he knew the sun would rise each morning, that the children would sing even if the barn was on fire and that murder was a necessary evil. *We Silvis must not let him see our mouths.*

He blinked as the female gurgled in a choking way that shook his roots. Did he have a mouth? He'd never used it here, in the dark world. That was really the only world he remembered with any clarity. There were dreams that visited him when he rested. They were... made of magic. A yellowness would glow all around and he could move his head to look up at the blue blanket they lived beneath. Beautiful dreams.

The warmth of the crystal's pull returned as the wizard fiddled with things behind his back. His body hummed as he became the conduit to feed the ever-hungry gem. That was all that mattered. That, and to not show the powerful creature his mouth. Everything else could wait. Of course it could. It could sit in the darkness.

Tymph focused on that humming feeling as his life drained away yet again. He could almost drown out the sounds of the female as the sorcerer stripped the layers of bark away to find her core. Only that would suffice to make the paper he would later write on while burning Tymph's skin to call forth a wicked energy. He visualized his lips pressing together so they would blend in with the bark and stay hidden. *The great wizard musn't see them. He can never know. The sun cannot rise if he sees them.* Tymph rested as his body hummed, as his bark was peeled and burned, as the sorcerer chanted and brought words and symbols from another realm into this world.

TYMPH WATCHED THE powerful wizard write. He'd ignored Tymph for a long time, coming and going up the stairs three dozen times at least. He no longer drained the great tree. He ignored him. Completely. Somehow, the Silvis pulled himself out the realm of insanity. His hunger was near the tipping point where it became an annoyance that he grew used to, like a long scratch-session that eventually numbed the bark.

The wizard had many lanterns surrounding his desk and on shelves, bringing more light than Tymph had experienced in a century. It hurt his eyes, but it was a beautiful sight. With his gifted vision, he could see the book the wizard slaved over. He presumed the words were the same language the wizard chanted all those years. He couldn't read it. There were tiny, naked women drawn in the edges like characters in the sky. He recognized a form of astronomy.

The human jumped up often to check his notes, flipping the book back and forth. Tymph realized there were three, separate parts. Each topic he wrote had a segment in all three parts, so there was much turning of pages.

Thick, flesh-colored pages made of Silvis core.

I'm going to kill you. Tymph was at peace with the thought. Once, long ago, he actually considered it wrong to kill. But after all the murders he had seen to create this book, he knew the powerful wizard must be stopped.

None ever returned to us.

A tear fell. He let it. Not that he could move to catch it. How many souls of the Silvis had been forced here by the power of the crystal for their last incarnation, never to fulfill their duty? If they could be called back, the powerful human would have brought them back to kill and core them again and again. It was difficult for him to find a new Silvis soul. Tymph thought it strange that the wizard didn't core him as well. But, he realized, the health of the sorcerer was also tied to the crystal. And the crystal was tied to Tymph.

So it was up to Tymph to destroy the crystal, the great wizard or himself.

But how? It consumed his every waking moment. He wasted precious weeks following each idea through to a miserable ending that caused the sorcerer great pain and brought him his first pleasure in countless years. Enjoyable, but not fruitful. Tymph went through his files, looking carefully at each noted item:

He has only a portion of my name- that should help me break the Awakening, surely.

He thinks I'm immobile, body, mind and spirit. He has only one of the three. How to use that?

My voice can call to magic.

Tymph grimaced. That was the hardest to understand, the part that made him feel a failure to Gaia. His birthright was to call on the earth magic as his own. Yet.... He had been able to bring forth nothing during the times he sat alone in the stone cell. *Nothing.* From the base of his soul he'd called, sang, chanted and dared to scream, yet no tendrils of magic curled through the earth to answer him.

The trap might not have captured his mind and soul, but it completely controlled his magic. Tymph had hoped the spell would faulter if he lived from one Solstice to the next. He slowed his breath and his metabolism for months but it had also slowed the fill of the crystal, so much so that the wizard used fire to end that incarnation and recapture his soul at the following Solstice. But still, he thought something was there. If he could stay alive for a full year and see the longest night, he might end this circle of complete subjugation.

He would prefer, however, to find a way to kill the wizard; to move his branch-hands down from their eternal stretch and wrap his lithe fingers around that thin, white neck; to throttle him with slow, deep squeezes followed by a shake so violent the wizard's brain would rattle in the skull; to *say their names, a* call to witness for every Silvis who had been caught and butchered in this hole connected to hell while...

Tymph pushed away the thought. He had already lost too much time indulging in such fantasies. Now, it was time to put the clues together and end this.

HE FAILED. AFTER more Awakenings than he dared count, Tymph failed to kill the wizard, destroy the crystal, or end his torturous cycle of life.

It had taken scores of Awakenings for him to accept it. There was a stubbornness in his makeup that refused to admit defeat. It was a part of his core to believe good would always outfox, overcome and blatantly outmaneuver evil.

But the great wizard wrote a second book.

This one was, to his distress, something Tymph could read. *MALLEUS MALEFICARUM, Maleficas & earum hæresim, ut phramea potentissima conerens,* in the widespread language of Latin. And for the first time, Tymph had a name for the evil man that fed off his soul: Henricus Institoris.

It was a detailed legal and theoretical argument for the absolute extermination of witches. And it went beyond the arguments of *why,* delving straight into the arena of *how to uncover the Beast hidden within a woman.*

THE HAMMER OF WITCHES
which destroyeth WITCHES and their heresy
as with a two-edged sword

Tymph witnessed as the torture practiced on Silvis in his stone prison was inked out as an unholy *manual.*

A MANUAL! His soul howled. It came unhinged from his body and slammed against the shell of bark and leaf that trapped him. It pushed against his skull and crashed into his roots, seeking a release.

But Tymph found only an eternal shackle of everything he knew.

He could not defeat this creature of a man. It was beyond his ability, alone and unaided, to overcome and conquer.

Tymph strained his vision as never before when the sorcerer carried the evil book up the stairs. He followed him, on some strange, ethereal level, far beyond his gifts of vision alone, a part of him detaching and hounding the trail of evil as it went above ground, was handed to another who pressed into service a myriad of skilled hands that copied and distributed the book throughout the lands of many countries.

It spread like a plague.

TYMPH FOUND HIMSELF looking at his own hull of a body, outside of it, holding to the edge of the cell. A single candle glowed as the wizard leaned against the tree, crowing his victory and his hatred of women as he ejaculated against the tree.

Tymph could not win. The truth settled into his limbs and bark as clearly as the sun rises each morning. He could not defeat this creature, and the great evil of this man would destroy the world.

Tymph accepted it.

It was possible. The Good of all could lose the war against evil.

As the wizard pulled his spent frame back, Tymph saw rather than felt the leaves of his canopy fall away, pulled toward the wizard. But instead of a gentle sway in their final release, the joining with earth, which was the season of autumn, each leaf drove itself into the ancient body of the sorcerer, slicing him apart with clean cuts like a hot knife moving through cold butter.

He was free. Gaia intervened, and at last, he was free.

Tymph returned to his body and moved slowly up the stairs, dazed, numb. He struggled to accept the light of day when he exited his world and discovered that a place of dawn and dusk occurred beyond his dreams. He lived on the sides of roads and stone pathways, watching people move, never speaking with any soul, even those he knew saw him. The witches burned all across the countryside, in nation after nation, their screams mixing in Tymph's soul with those of the Silvis lost to the wizard.

Tymph was the first and only Silvis to die of a sorrow so complete that it outshone the sun. His lesson scoured his soul, but worse than that. Far worse. It broke his heart. Gaia needed him to see what he never thought possible.

For it was there that Gaia herself walked, fearful and alone. It was there that he must choose to go to join her fight, or race away into oblivion.

Excerpt from Cora Belle Blue:

Stories from Beyond the Portal: Who is killing the Fae?

By Ruth Souther

A Fae Warrior is charged with treason and her punishment is banishment to Chicago, IL. As Cora Belle from Blue Water Tribe attempts to assimilate into the human realm, she meets an array of Fae beings who are also banished but are now turning up deceased in a most uncommon manner. She has no interest in solving the mystery until Elvis the Dragon disappears. Can she find and rescue her friend before he, too, winds up dead? (A Cozy Mystery of the Fae Persuasion)

Chapter 1

The portal opened and I was unceremoniously thrown through the shimmering rainbow light. For one airborne moment, I was featherlike, floating through the brightness, my breath caught in my throat. I had no fear for what lay beyond. I am a warrior, after all, and it is my nature to be prepared for anything.

Perhaps, though, I should be afraid: I was not prepared for banishment. When I was seized in the early morning, shortly after rising, and hurled into the Netherlands, I was shocked.

To surrender my life for my Queen, yes.

To be outcast from all that was familiar, no.

While it was true, I had defied my Queen's orders, I had believed Queen Penarddun would understand and forgive me. To be so incorrect stunned me.

The brief trip through the bright and colorful prism ended and I bounced off something rough, grainy and pain-producing. My face smacked full into the coarse material and skin ripped away. I fell backwards, landing on my duff, the sting of skinned knuckles registering as I tried to break my fall. My sword whacked me in the head as the hard leather sword casing caught and twisted on my back. Blood ran from the scratches on my face and my whole body ached from the impact.

Disoriented, I looked up. And up, and up, and up.

I had not just hit a wall, but a building. An enormous structure such as I had never seen. I sat still, staring upward at a night sky obliterated by a multitude of garish lights. It was dark and yet it was not dark.

Beyond the roofline that had attacked me, there were many more, taller structures glinting reflections of each other. The edifices were horrible glaring masses of glass and metal, although some had rough brick and mortar exteriors, as the one I smashed into with such force.

Beneath me was more of the rough material fashioned into a walkway where not a nick of grass, or anything else green, could be found. The surface went from the edge of the building to the rounded curb, and the curb went into a broad and busy street, which was at least twenty lengths wide. And even with nightfall, there were clumps of metal monsters whizzing past each other in clouds of noxious fumes and bright white lights.

The chaos, the smell, the deforestation: what was this awful place?

My head swam and my gut lurched. I thought I might vomit right there on that spot. Fighting back the urge, but not really knowing why as the street was already filthy, I staggered to my feet and held onto the very wall that had sent me flying.

"Those bloody evil bastards," I muttered in reference to the Glas Ddyfrhaech Llyth Council. "Where on this good Earth did they send me?" I glanced over my shoulder. "Is this not Earth but another place in the Universe, some hideous realm that is made of pure ugliness? By Danu's blood, where am I?"

No one responded even though there were people all about, walking along the path. Some gave me a sideways glance and stepped as far away from me as they could. Others stared outright, suspicious stares, curious stares, fearful stares.

I stared right back, casting Fae magic at them so they would only see a female leaning against the building and not an armed, blue-skinned, angry and confused Faerie spewing a language they did not understand. It was dark, nightfall, I presumed, and not just some human-induced fabrication for effect. I was not in a tunnel or beneath ground though I could not see any stars for the constant glare from the metal monsters and buildings. I turned slowly and pressed my back against the rough surface to support my shaking knees. The broadsword strapped to my back dug into the flesh between my shoulders and gave me a small

amount of comfort, just to know it was there.

The noise was nearly unbearable. I held my hands to my ears but could not block out the hateful sounds around me. I do not shed tears easily but I confess my eyes misted as I felt all I cared for was lost to me. Hunching closer to the wall, I lowered my head and wondered what I was to do with myself in this goddess-forsaken place.

I had sworn to protect Queen Penarddun with my blood, and I have done so faithfully for over a thousand years. Yet, here I was in exile. However doubtful, it was one I did not regret no matter the punishment. The grief in my heart was not in regard to what I had done. It was the pain and sorrow etched onto the face of my Queen. I caused that, and yet, I know in my deepest place that she understood why. Perhaps she even agreed on my actions. She could never say that, and she could not save

me from this exile. Or would not.

She stood mute as she watched while I was stripped of my honor as Captain of the Queen's guard and left with only the clothing I had on, the sword strapped to my back, and the twin daggers hidden inside my boots. I heard a small cry, I think, I want to believe was from Queen Penarddun as I was forced through the threshold into this ugly and loud place with rude buildings that drew blood.

And now it was done. I was here in this hateful place to suffer endless torture for the next hundred years. Anger boiled up and my strength returned.

Cursing, I stood away from the wall.

"Even though I am at Hu Gadain's door," I said, straightening my tunic and my sword. "I will not surrender."

"Not the Otherworld," a high-pitched voice spoke next to me. "Although, I admit, there are times when it feels like hell."

I turned and saw a young woman dressed in a short, plaid skirt, not unlike the Highlanders, though her vocals were not at all like the Scots. She had long hair curling all about her face and shoulders that appeared a burnished copper in the glare surrounding us. Many things piercing her skin. Nose, ears, eyebrows, lower lip, little rods and hoops everywhere. The metal glinted ominously in the harsh lights of this world. I wondered if they were some sort of weapons cleverly disguised as decoration.

Although she spoke English, it was not Britannia's proper speak. I could still understand her. I knew many languages, could place many strange accents, but this one remained a mystery. It appeared that she also understood me, but I switched from the Fae tongue to Britannia. It would not take long for me to pick up the local dialect, I had only to hear it a few times before I could mimic these crude mortals.

"What is this place?" I snapped.

"She-Caw-Ga." She spoke with a soft lilt. I still did not know from whence this accent came. Further, I did not know what region was implied.

"I do not know She-Caw-Ga. Would you enlighten me?"

"Oh, my dear." The girl smiled and the metal on her face reflected like tiny mirrors. "They didn't even tell you where you were going? That is so not fair. And from the looks of you…." She paused to scan up and down my body. "They did nothin' to get you ready, either. You must've been a difficult banishment."

"It was rather sudden," I replied with a tightness in my throat.

"I suppose it was all lies, right? That's what they all say," she drawled. "But, truly, we shouldn't stand out here on the street. It's a mite risky. Let's go inside where we can sit and talk a bit." She reached for my elbow.

"I go nowhere with you." I jerked my arm away from her hovering hand. "Leave me."

"That's not a good idea, Chica. You're in North America now and that's a long way from home."

North America. She-Caw-Ga.

Danu save me, I was in the United States of America. Chicago, Illinois, to be exact.

And yes, I had heard of the filthy place. Others of our kind had traveled here, but not I. My Queen did not like cities and rarely strayed out of the Welsh countryside, let alone to a place across the big water.

I peered over my shoulder, suspicious now of my surroundings. Whatever confusion I had was gone, evaporated by the immediate need to secure my situation. Those who had initiated my exile had chosen this location with purpose in the hopes I would not survive.

Amidst the raucous sounds of the metal monsters and the buzzing of the fake lights, I heard rustling, stealthy footsteps and quiet but ragged breathing. My sensitive nose picked up putrid animal scents, rotting garbage, and human urine.

These offensive odors came from beyond the corner of the building where a break between the giant structures was swathed in darkness. I drew my sword and fell into a fighting stance, my blade held in my left hand, balanced on my right arm.

"Oh, my, there's no need for violence." The young woman held up both hands. "Those are just the wolves coming to see who popped through."

Five figures emerged from the shadows but they were not wolves. These folk stood on two feet. I could not see their faces, but mixed with the animal scent was human. I knew of shapeshifters, however every last one left Fae alone. Most creatures did. There were very few who could fight Fae magic and have any hope to win, and all were grateful if they escaped with their lives.

The five stopped in their tracks. One said, "Nice sword, never seen one like that before, wouldn't want it to get scratched." His voice was gravely and I could not tell if he offered compliment or caution.

"And you never will again," I snarled as I brandished my blade in front of me.

My sword was cast just for me, inscribed with my magic, answering to my hand alone. The blade was etched with the ancient symbols of my people, Glas Ddyfrhaech Llyth, and the hilt was wrapped in painted leather. It glinted dangerously in the beacon falling from an overhead post.

"Could you please put that thing away?" The young woman waved at the five to stay where they were, not that they were advancing. They stood close together with their arms hanging loosely at their sides, perhaps getting ready to attack, perhaps getting ready to run.

"No." My tone was as sharp as the edge of my blade.

"Hey, forgive me for not introducing myself." The girl brushed the top of her head with one hand before reaching out for a handshake.

I ignored her. I do not like to be touched.

"My name is Brazil. We've gotten off on the wrong foot." Brazil smiled, showing pointed teeth, with slightly elongated canines, reminiscent of the Scottish Silver Mountain Tribe. "It's starting to snow, let's go inside. You really do look cold. Kinda turning blue, there, Chica." There was a touch of urgency in her voice.

I glanced at my hands. Against the little flecks of snow, the blue was quite apparent. Before I could answer there was another flurry of sound, wings flapping, big wings. A dry, dusty scent filtered down and caused my gaze to rise. As I looked up, the pack of five shuffled a bit closer. Palm out, I lifted my right hand in warning, and raised the sword into a slashing stance.

They stopped moving.

"Really, we need to go inside." The whites of Brazil's eyes were glowing in the dark but she managed another smile and again I glimpsed those elongated canines.

"And why is that?" I stared at her with growing awareness of the dangers of this treacherous place. The vague scent lifting from her body had a hint of fear to it.

"Because you are causing quite the commotion, and everyone is curious. And, trust me, you don't want to meet everyone just yet."

The flapping noise stopped. I became aware of bird-like creatures gliding through the light flurry. They were larger than a human but not in appearance as were the shapeshifters.

"Who are they?" "The Simurghs." "Good omens."

"Not here, they aren't." Brazil glanced over her shoulder as three Simurgh landed on the opposite side of us. "Remember, these folk have been banished from their homelands as well, for whatever reason. I'm never told the reasons. I hardly think that's fair, but I don't make the rules. I just attend to the gateway and try to help."

Her voice was getting shriller as she watched the new arrivals.

Both front and back of the walkway were now blocked. If I were to escape, I would have to cross the path of those metal monsters whizzing along the road. At that moment, I realized that not a single human being was passing by us. They were paused in clumps up and down the street, unmoving, staring into windows or frozen into postures. The metal ones kept moving but not one individual glanced our way.

"Please, trust me. I know that is nearly beyond your understanding, but I will explain everything inside. There will be many other gawkers if we don't move along, and things could get ugly."

Brazil saw me look askance at the humans and added, "We wouldn't want someone to get hurt, would we?"

"It would very much depend on whom that someone was." I curled my lip in defiance. "They will not attack me."

"Maybe not, but they will start attacking each other and then, hoo boy, innocent humans get hurt."

"You are not human." It was not a question. I knew she was not. "Are you Silver Mountain Tribe?"

I squinted at the girl, trying to see past the clothing. I could sense nothing from her, but that could just be a clever cover. Silver Mountain folk were very good at shielding. Her skin tone was coppery in color and did not match the silvery white of the Mountains.

She did not smell like Mountain Fae. She smelled like deep forest and running water. And she did not behave like a Fae.

Brazil shook her head. "No. I will tell you all about me, and them, and all the others, if you will please just come with me." Her anxiety was frothing to the top.

In the distance, I heard yet another unusual sound, a slithering, scales on rough surface sound. The smell was sewer-like. I did not want to see where that came from. Perhaps Brazil was right and we should adjourn to somewhere inside.

The snow was getting heavier and my clothing was getting wet. Since I had nothing else to change into, it would seem pertinent to get out of the weather. I nodded and sheathed my sword, and hoped I was not making a mistake.

With a huge sigh of relief, Brazil pushed past the three Simurghs. They took a step back from us but glared at me through hungry yellow eyes.

"Try it," I hissed at them and they fell back another step. The shapeshifters stood fast to their spot. I did not see the scaly one.

Nothing happened, not one of them challenged me. I cannot express my disappointment that there was no skirmish to be had.

I really was in a fighting mood.

Brazil opened the door, which jingled happily at our entrance, and escorted me into a store of sorts. There were racks and stands and tables filled with books of dizzying sizes, shapes and colors. There were big pictures posted all along the walls, pretty little baskets of bottles, and boxes of writing paper and pens. I didn't know what some of the things were for, but they were everywhere, and everything was bright.

Very bright. I shielded my eyes from the glare and slowly moved my gaze along the shelves. There were people wandering through the aisles, thumbing through books, or studiously reading glossy magazine pages.

The scent of paper, glue and wood, of cleansers and paint and the acrid scent of sealants gave me a piercing ache mid-temple. Layered upon that was the smell of humans, their sweat and blood, their perfumes and lotions, the overall scent of their bodies was overpowering.

I felt assaulted on every level, every sense and was made dizzy by it all.

Steadying myself against an empty table, I attempted to clear my head. Instinctively, I drew a deep breath, and that was a frightful mistake. It lent to my overall queasiness.

"Are you alright?" Brazil reached as if to touch me and then quickly withdrew her hand at my glare.

"This place stinks and the light hurts my eyes. I do not like it here." "I understand." Her voice was sympathetic.

I dislike sympathy. Pulling further away from her, I took in another deep breath and this one brought in a new scent. A heady aroma that dismissed all others came flowing through the air and I turned toward it. It made my mouth water. It was rich, with a hint of nuts and cinnamon, and hot milk.

Leaving Brazil, I followed the wafting stream and arrived at a station with a glass case filled with pastries.

The young male behind the counter stared at me. The little plaque pinned to his shirt said 'Devon'.

"Nice costume." Devon nodded in approval. "Those ears look real. I've never seen them put on quite so, er, perfectly. And your hair and skin, man you really went all out. How long did it take to get that shade? And where'd you get the dye? I tried some from the Halloween Shop but it just didn't come out that good. I was going for green, though, because I...."

His voice trailed off into an uncomfortable silence as I gave him my best 'I-could-kill-you-before-you-blink' glare.

Clearing his throat, Devon asked, "So, what can I get for you?" I approved of his decision to get on with the business at hand. "Whatever it is that created that divine smell."

"Coffee?"

"Is that what scent is in the air?"

"Well, I guess. Unless it's the Chai, but it's probably...." Again he stopped at my expression.

"What kind?" He pointed at a sign on the wall behind him with a dazzling list of drinks. I had no idea what any of them were.

"The one I am smelling," I snapped.

Devon shook his head and mumbled, "Foreigners." With a sigh, "Both the coffee and the tea have cinnamon; I just want to make sure you get what you want. So is it the coffee, for sure?"

"Coffee." He was starting to annoy me. "Does it have cinnamon in it?" "If it's the Hazelnut..."

"Yes, that."

"Okay, what size?"

He pointed to the sign again. I pointed at a stack of paper cups. "Cream or sugar?"

"Er...no?"

"Okay." Devon nodded and filled a cup, snapped a lid on it, and said "$3.75."

He meant money, and I had none. "So that'll be $3.75."

Money.

I had none.

But now I badly wanted that drink, if only to hurl it back at him.

"Ma'am?"

My attention returned to the young man. I met his eyes, stared hard, whispered a simple spell of glamour, and handed him three folded napkins from the nasty metal dispenser on the counter.

"Thank you," he mumbled, and put the napkins in his cash register. "Indeed." I smiled and walked away with my drink.

I sat down at the first table and holding the hot drink between my hands, contemplated my situation. Brazil plopped down in the opposite chair. "Well, it would seem you are much better at takin' care of yourself than I would have imagined."

"You could have assisted me."

"I could've, yes, but you've made it pretty clear you don't want my help."

"Who are you? What are you?" "I told you, I'm Brazil."

"Of what tribe?" I sipped at the drink and burned my mouth. Swearing, I sat it down and stared at my blue hands gripping the cup. My fingernails were darker, nicely manicured. The Queen's guard always maintained the best appearance possible.

"No tribe. It's just my mother and my sisters and me." She broke into a song that was neither chant nor ballad: "We are family, my mother and my sisters and me...."

I closed my eyes, rubbed my forehead and tried to shut out the sound of her screechy voice. What was I to do now? Though I had my weapons, what good are they? I had no currency, no place to go, and no way of knowing where to start.

Fae cruelty was legendary, but this surpassed all torture I had ever witnessed. I decided at that moment I would rather take the torment of a thousand poisonous stings than be outcast from Faerie. What was I supposed to do? What had all those other banished Fae done?

I was sickened to think I had been part of sending others, however deserving, into the same fate I now faced. And as I thought of those others, I realized how many of them had not returned once their sentences were complete. I began to count them, those we had shoved through the shimmering rainbow light, and those that had come back.

Out of hundreds, perhaps a dozen had returned. What had happened to the rest of them?

I brought the cup to my lips, prepared to be soothed by the cooling drink. And immediately spewed it across the table. It was the most foulest of foul tasting brews I had ever consumed.

If those lost had tasted coffee, it was a certain bet they were dead, done in by the same poison as in my cup. I leaped to my feet, sword plucked from its scabbard, ready to behead young Devon for the attempt on my life.

"It would just be so much better if you would not pull that big ole blade out amongst the humans. It tends to scare them, even if Devon does think it's part of a costume." She was mopping up the spilled coffee with paper napkins as she spoke.

"Again, please put that damned thing away before you draw any more attention to yourself." Arching her brows at the sword, she added, "If you do not hide your weapon, someone will call the police."

"I care nothing about the human enforcers. I do not answer to their law."

"You should care about the 'enforcers' because they will certainly care about you. More than one of your type has landed in the hokey pokey, and believe me, it is not an easy task to get you out of jail." Brazil leveled an amber gaze at me. "And with your attitude, I'm not too sure I'd want to bail you out."

"I do not need your help."

"Oh, please." Brazil leaned forward, arms crossed on the table in front of her. Her blouse was cut low and it seemed as if her breasts would fall out but somehow didn't, staying tucked into the tight fabric. "You need to take it down a notch. Whatever you did to get banished, it couldn't have been nice. You're here, and even if you don't know it yet, you need me."

"I ask again, who are you?" My tone was cold, but I replaced my weapon in its casing and sat on the edge of my chair, though my heart thumped with an irregular beat.

"I am a gatekeeper. I keep an eye on all the nasties that come through." She cocked her head to one side. "You being one of those nasties, and yet, you are different. Not like the others. Nothing has come through in over six months through order of the High Council, and yet, here you are. So, the question I have now is, who the hell are you?"

"No one." I avoided her gaze.

"Yeah, sure. What is it about you? Hmmm. Well, it could be the quick use of that ginormous sword that sets you apart, kinda makes you unique. Most come across with no clue, let alone in full gear. Most are scared witless even if they've been naughty enough to get tossed out on their behinds.

"There've been a few true criminals pass our way, but mostly just those who need to be taught a lesson. But the question is, what did you do and why do you need a lesson? Or are you a criminal? You seem fairly well set upon the idea that you should show me the way rather than me showing you. Interesting." Her voice was now a different pitch, lower, almost a purr.

Brazil smiled broadly at my raised eyebrows and I caught sight of the canines. There was no further doubt that they were full out fangs. The glimpse made me sit up straight. Never mind what was I. What in ocean's tides was she? Brazil may be a sanctioned custodian, but she was much more than that.

I stared at her lips, now closed but still curved upwards in a full, red smile. I tried to convince myself that my imagination had taken control but in that split moment, with the overhead lights, I saw amber cat eyes and a hint of tufted ears beneath the red hair.

I wanted to look under her skirt to see if she had a tail, but that would be rude.

"You are not what you appear."

"True," Brazil returned to that young girl voice, letting it drizzle all around me like warm summer rain. "Hey, there, y'all, welcome to Books on State! If there's something in particular you're looking for, just let me know, I'm here to serve you." She was talking to a couple passing by our table as she pointed to her name tag and gave them a friendly grin, minus the fangs.

The couple nodded, gave a little hand wave of thanks, but no thanks, and shuffled off.

In a blink of the eye, the bright-eyed, flirty girl was gone again. Brazil was back to the direct approach, if a bit too wordy for my liking. "And neither are you."

With a narrowed gaze that scanned me from head to feet, Brazil made a clucking noise. "You obviously had no warning, no preparation, no instructions, nothing to let you know you were going to get the boot. My guess is you were a head honcho of some kind and they didn't want to give you a chance to kick somebody's ass." She pointed a finger at me. "And you look like you could kick some royal ass."

I flinched and she saw it.

"Ah. You had something to do with the royal family. Are you a princess?

Is that it? A real, live princess?"

I remained mute, my lips pinched together.

"Hmmm, not a princess. How about Queen? Duchess? Empress?"

With each word, my mouth involuntarily quirked to one side in a sneer. She was grasping, now, and it was starting to irritate me all over again. I would take her head just to shut her up if it would not be too terribly messy, considering where we were. With that thought, my fingers flexed as if I would snatch up a dagger.

Brazil saw the involuntary movement and laughed with delight. "You are priceless, darlin'. I'm going to enjoy taking care of you."

"I don't need anyone to take care of me." I rose from my seat.

"You can't go about like that, all blue and swinging that big hunk of metal at everyone." Brazil observed. "You truly will end up in the loony bin, if you don't kill someone first."

I started to say my weapon was not 'just a hunk of metal' but thought better of it as she also stood. I realized for the first time that she was taller than I. For Fae, I stood above others, but not in the human realm.

There, I was at least half a head shorter, and sometimes much more. I didn't like being at a disadvantage and took a few steps backwards to give us an even field.

"Oh, come on," Brazil coaxed, following my steps forward. "I'm sorry if I spooked you but I really am here to help."

"I don't want or need your help." "Yes, you do."

I didn't. I chose to ignore her and walk away.

"Wait!" She caught my arm and we both froze. Me, because I felt claws on my skin, even through my sleeve, and she, because she touched a Fae guard without asking. My reflexes took over and I grabbed her wrist, twisted her arm behind her until she yelped and was forced to her knees. It was then I noticed everyone in the area was staring at us. I released Brazil and dropped both hands to my sides to show I was not going to harm her.

"Just let me help you." Brazil climbed to her feet. "You don't have to like me or trust me. Just let me do my job."

"Leave me alone or next time, I will kill you." With that parting shot, I walked away from her. As I was going out the door, I heard her sigh, "Oh, Yamanya, help us, this one is going to be a pain in the ass, that's for sure."

Excerpt from Appalachia Tales
By Keri Goble Billick

Wax, Frank and Marley
July 16, 84 NE

The sky was a dark mix of black and red. As day slowly transitioned to night the silhouette of a black tower could be seen in the distance. It seemed almost out of place this far up in the mountains. It loomed above the landscape like a relic from times long since passed. It was lit by giant spotlights at its base.

The cries of hundreds filled the air with a sorrowful din. The sound they created was an unending hymn of woe that seemed to physically weigh down all who heard it. There was great pain and gnashing of teeth. Atop the tower was a man dressed in black and silver armor. Close inspection of the man revealed a chain mesh mask riveted to his forehead.

It fell in the shape of a skull over his scarred face.

His eyes were cold and black. They were deep pits behind the tarnished and worn mask. He surveyed his kingdom intently, listening to the song of sorrow with a pleasant smirk. He stood satisfied, proud and tall.

Deep and erratic scars covered his face. They traced chaotic paths through the lines and valleys of his grizzled visage, spreading to every visible inch of skin.

To his left was a crouching man, nearly naked and frightfully thin. This emaciated shell of a man looked off into the distance and pointed to a crowd below.

In an arena lined with skulls, two figures battled with weapons of steel. Sparks flew as they hacked away at each other, every blow meant to kill. In the end, it was the female who stood victorious after plunging her blade into the eye socket of her opponent. She wore a dark red hood which hid her features. Slowly she turned to the king, high atop the tower, and saluted by raising her right fist into the air. She reached up to pull the hood from her face.

Wax rolled out of bed with a thud, gasping from the fright of the dream and the surprise of her fall. Her mother, Shannan, began to call her Wax when she was just a baby. She said you could follow Heidi's mood with the moon. The waxing moon seemed to be when she was at her very best. The moon last night was at one quarter and waning. It was July 16, 84 NE -- 151 years to the day since the first detonation of an atomic weapon.

The sun had just come up as Wax reflexively began to do her morning exercises. Her pace was quick as she breezed through fifty sit-ups and began to do leg lifts. She looked forward to next month in the Franklin settlement when Bill the Mage would change her training schedule. She did not like to do calisthenics, and she was already in a foul mood this morning. Her dreams had upset her.

"Mreow," squawked Marley, her sleek black cat. Marley was slow to wake and not at all pleased to have to move from his comfy pillow. He jumped from the bed right on to Wax's tightened stomach.

"OW," Wax coughed. "Do you mind? It's bad enough I have to deal with your screaming every morning! Do you have to jump on me, too?" "Mrrph," said Marley. He pressed his cold nose against her cheek and

hopped to the floor.

Wax heard a voice in her head, "Why you are grumpy, Wax?" The voice was a projection from her fluffy black cat, Frank. Using a technique learned from her aunt Brenda, Wax was able to both speak to and hear the projected voice of those she had a close bond with. Frank was her familiar, they had been talking for many years.

There were those who thought she was just talking to herself. But anyone who understood the Angel Tides knew better. She routinely spoke to both Frank and Marley. Marley, however, was far too stubborn to project the voice. Instead, he left it to Wax to learn his language.

"I had bad dreams," said Wax, "Plus, it's Monday, and I don't want to train today. I would rather sleep in." She flopped over on to her tummy and began to do push-ups.

"Mrear Mupfph," said Marley.

"Yes, Wax. Marley is right. Grandpa is gone. You don't have training today." Frank let out an audible chirp as he finished his sentence. He rarely made a sound. When he did it was usually used as punctuation.

Wax stopped mid push up. She sprang to her feet with a thrust of her arms and began to jump around the room with glee. Frank joined in, running around her feet while Marley watched the two of them doing their silly dance. Wax stopped suddenly.

"You know what we should do, then?" She paused for suspense. "We should make a picnic and go up into the foothills. We can get some sun!" She began to gather things in a yellow backpack.

First, a journal, followed by some nail polish, her favorite black pen, chop sticks, colored pencils, an iPod, hair ties, a bag of catnip, six feet of a small cotton rope with a coin weighing down one end, a periwinkle Sharpie, index cards, five silver coins and a pocket knife.

"Ok, let's hit the kitchen. Then we can take off." Wax was in a much better mood than when she first awoke. Her dream was already fading, and the news she would not have to spend the day working to stay in shape was intoxicating. Next month could not come soon enough.

She bounded from her room, through the common room, and into the kitchen. The common room of the cottage was sparsely decorated with a few items which were oriental in design. In the center was a red futon folded up into a couch. On the east wall was an antique sewing table with some incense, a gong and several small statues of Buddha.

Once in the kitchen, Wax crammed some bread and cheese into her pack, zipped it up, and headed outside. She stopped in the doorway when she heard her familiar's voice in her head again.

"What about your bokken?" Frank asked. He pawed at two cherry wood swords on a stand in the common room beside the sewing table. On a shelf above them was a pair of katana in red and gold scabbards with a cherry blossom crest. These were the swords of her mother.

"No, silly, I'm not training," said Wax, "It's a fun day."

"But Grandpa says you should always have..." Frank was cut off.
"Grandpa is not here, Boo Bug," said Wax, "So he doesn't have to know, does he?"

"Mraeow," said Marley, as the three headed out the door and set off to the east.

All was calm to the west of Clayton. A tiny finger of white light began to dance and crackle. As the glowing tear expanded, dark figures could be seen in its center. When the dancing lights faded, two men stood where once there was no one. With them was the stench of rotting meat. One man was in black armor. He was tall with dark skin and long dark hair pulled into a top knot. The dark man's armor was shiny and unblemished. His boots seemed larger and heavier than they should be. He had a carriage proud and wide with no sign of confusion or hesitation.

He was called Aaron.

"Is this the right town, Joshua?" asked Aaron.

The man to his left was dressed in black and blood-red robes. He was thin, with long hair and abnormally large eyes. Closer inspection of his eyes revealed a dance of color with no discernible shape or pattern. This man, however, was not Joshua. His name was Kelvin Bane, and his power was devastating.

"Affirmative, Aaron. This is Clayton." said Joshua. The voice came from a giant black sword strapped to Aaron's back.

The handsome weapon had a very long two-handed grip with red jewels on the hilt that seemed to glow slightly. The shimmering black blade emanated life energy all its own. From sword tip to the end of the pommel it measured exactly six feet.

"Good," said Aaron, "Let's not waste time." He began walking briskly toward Clayton. His steps were strong and self-assured. He exuded the confidence of a man who knew no fear and had a clear vision of his mission.

Kelvin followed, weaving as he walked and muttering to himself. "Going to the south. To the south. To the south." His head ticked back and forth with his mutterings. "Time to play. Yes, good fun. Play play play." He stopped mid stride and looked to his left at no one. "OF COURSE I AM READY!"

Aaron looked back at him shaking his head, one eyebrow raised inquisitively. "Bane!" he said sternly, "Keep up, or suffer." His stride did not break as he spoke. He smiled to himself, amused by the psychosis of his traveling companion.

"You mean keep up AND suffer," muttered Kelvin, "Nothing is for free, you see. Nothing. Nothing. Nothing. It all costs. Always pay with the pain. With great power comes..." he looked off to the left again, "GREAT PAIN!"

Soon, the two men and elegant intelligent weapon were at the edge of Clayton. The village walls had long since been dismantled after the peace that had been established in the Southern Free Zone. They looked around at the village inhabitants going about their business. Some folks were tending gardens containing every vegetable imaginable. Others were building or repairing many of the town's structures. Near a church, a blue-eyed woman read to a gathering of children.

People seemed far too trusting of strangers in this odd, clean place. They moved about with pleasant looks upon their faces, very different than the realm of these warrior visitors. The smell of their homeland was fading, replaced by that of nectar and goodness.

"Soon, these peasants will be the first to see how life will be under their future leader," said Aaron.

Wax sat down heavily upon a rock and dug through her backpack. She wiped the bottom of her feet off on patches of grass as she searched through the yellow pouch. Marley sniffed around for a smooth, warm rock on which to take a mid-morning nap. After a few seconds of debate, he circled a rock three times and slowly laid down on its sun warmed surface. Frank just stared at Wax.

"Why stopped?" asked Frank.

"This is the spot where I am going to paint my toes," said Wax, as she pulled the nail polish from her pack. "It's perfect, see?" She pointed down the hill to Clayton, now over a mile away. "We can see the whole village." She made a wide sweeping motion with her arm and propped her left foot up on the rock.

"Mrfph," said Marley before falling asleep.

"I still think you should have brought your bokken," said Frank in Wax's head. "Your grandpa said you should always have them with you." He gave a small head butt to her foot and chirped. "He says you will never know when trouble will pop up."

"Get serious," said Wax. "I have been training seven days a week as long as I can remember, and nothing has ever happened that would make me need my bokken." She propped up her left foot to begin painting. "Mom and Grandpa live in the past when they had to be armed twenty- four seven. It is a new era now, Boo Bug. Why should I arm myself for a day of rest and recreation?" She began to paint, little toe first.

"All I am saying is you never know," said Frank, "Your grandpa is a smart man and your Mommy has seen a lot of war rise from nothing." He sat gently and continued to look up at her with giant yellow eyes. "I think it is best to observe their wisdom."

"Cripes, Boo Bug," said Wax, "If you are going to lecture me all day, go home." She finished up the left foot and held up her work to exam the freshly painted digits. "If it makes you feel better, I promise I will take them with me everywhere from now on." She pulled her right foot up and dipped the brush into the polish.

"Yes," said Frank, "That does make me feel better." He smiled before pushing over the backpack and flattening out a nice place to lie down. He could not help but push the zipper with his nose, trying to get at the contents of the backpack. The catnip smelled very good to him.

Shannan was tending a garden when the two strangers entered town. She heard one of them ranting about pain, and the hair on the back of her neck stood on end. She quietly put down her hoe and walked off toward her cottage. She had known this day would come. It had only been a matter of time before those from north of the mysterious great wall made their move.

She hoped Wax was up so she could send her to tend to the day care children. She went over the path to be taken in her near future so she would not have to think when she got home. She remained perfectly calm and focused. Her movements were like fluid.

Shannan walked through the door and called out, "Wax?" There was no answer. She eased into the common room and removed her swords from their shelf, dropping sheaths to the floor. "Wax!?!" she screamed again, noticing Wax's bokken in their stands. As she was leaving through the kitchen, she noticed the missing loaves of bread from her counter. Wax had left already and neglected to take her swords. This was not a good sign.

Aaron stopped in the center square of the small town. By this time many had stopped what they were doing and gathered to greet the oddly dressed men. He looked around to see who any leaders here might be in case he needed to make an example of them. No one stood out until the tall blonde woman with swords in hand stepped into the street.

Shannan walked calmly toward the armored man. Her head was tilted forward slightly as she sized him up. The big sword would be cumbersome and clumsy against her katana. The thin man next to him had an aura about him that identified him as a caster. She whispered a low-level charm of arcane protection to give her enough time to take him down.

Aaron stepped forward and spoke.

"Now, Bane." said Aaron. "To my hand, Joshua." He held out his arm as the giant black sword rose from the mount on Aaron's back and positioned itself in his right hand. He pointed the bastard sword, with one hand, at Shannan as she quickened her approach. "Stay your swords, woman, lest you be taken by the hand of Aaron Achilles."

Kelvin Bane stepped forward and removed his robe. A strip was shaved up the center of his head. The runes tattooed there and down his naked body began to glow a bright red. "Citizens of Clayton," he said, "Fear not. What you are about to experience will not hurt." He smiled a sadistic grin and his eyes began to glow with a swirling red energy. "Much."

Shannan leapt into the air, screaming. The spell thrower was more powerful than his aura indicated. He was probably crazy. The leader still had to be taken out first. Hopefully his spell would take time to cast. She trained the blow of her right hand katana on the center of Aaron's head while preparing the left to deflect any blow he might send her way. Her hair waved behind her as she fell in an arc toward the darkly armored man and everything seemed to move in slow motion.

Aaron marveled at the height this woman had jumped into the air. Joshua moved Aaron's arm to counter her attack. It would be a shame to have to kill her. She would very much impress the master. His eyebrow arched again as Shannan's sword blurred to meet his own.

Wax put the earphones from her i-pod into her ears. She stripped to her bra and panties and laid back to catch the rays of the warm sun. The lyrics to a hundred-year-old song by a group called Blind Melon filled her head.

All I can say is that my life is pretty plain. I like watching the puddles gather rain.

She loved this music. She wished there were musicians alive today who produced such beautiful sounds. She rolled over on to her tummy only to face Marley on his rock. She kissed him on his cold wet nose and closed her eyes. She could have stayed this way forever but for the voice of her mother popping into her head.

"WAX!" said Shannan. "Go get Brenda and get help from the Franklin settlement. NOW!"

Wax was jolted to her feet. She looked around for a moment before realizing this order was telepathic. She grabbed her backpack, slid on her clothes and started towards Clayton, trying to think of how to respond to her mother.

BADOOM!!!!

Nearly a mile away, the former site of Clayton was a giant red glow of fire. She could see the shock wave leveling everything between her and her former home as it quickly ascended the foothills, radiating from ground zero. She was too shocked to react, not that it would have helped. She and the two cats were thrown head over tail when the wave hit.

She lay motionless for several minutes. Marley and Frank had landed on their feet but they were shaken. Marley pushed his wet nose into Wax's ear in an effort to wake her. He circled nervously, repeating the tactics but to no avail.

"Wax?" said Frank telepathically. "Wax, wake up." He began to panic. "WAKE UP!"

Wax stirred slightly and let out a low moan. She sat up holding her head with one hand and reflexively reaching to her waist to grab her bokken in the other. She became more aware of her surroundings when she noticed her bokken were not with her.

When she looked up to see what had happened, all she could see was a mushroom cloud rising to the heavens. The stem grew out of a smoldering crater where once stood her home, Clayton.

"Mommy?" she whimpered as a tear fell down her cheek.

Aaron stood in the center of the black crater, still holding Joshua to block the blow that would never come. Kelvin was no longer present. Aaron released the sword and looked around at the destruction as Joshua returned to his sheath. His armor still shone, showing no signs of what it had just been through.

He pulled a small silver marble from a pouch at his waist. Eyeing the marble closely he saw the tiny engraving Bagril Nilknarf had etched into it with acid. Using his heel, he dug a groove in the dirt and dropped the marble in. He then slid the loose dirt back over the small silver marble like a seed.

"Joshua." said Aaron. "Initiate return sequence." White light crackled, and they were gone.

Clayton was lost.

Excerpt from MMXVII

Druid|Ranger|Paladin
By Keri Goble Billick

PROLOGUE

From the journal of Melanie McAfee, Patient 011915.

Three
One is the base of all things. Our individual perspective originates in the one. No matter the name, all things begin with one. One is the base of all things.

Two is the recognition of other. A baby recognizes her father and they become two. Two separates and establishes duality. Night and day, heads and tails, hard and soft, wet and dry. One has an ever present equal opposite, and together they are two. Two is the recognition of other.

Three is the sacred number. It is the height, width and breadth of all things. It is the here in which one and two exist. It spreads like lattice throughout all creation always returning to itself. Three, in all its derivatives, has been, is and always will be. Three is a recurring theme one and two will recognize around them always. Three is the sacred number.

"Melanie?" Dr. Schnell asked after reading the section from her journal aloud. "Will you please explain to me, again, what that means?" "Um…" Melanie appeared distracted and avoided eye contact. "What now? Explain one, two and three?"

She tilted her head in thought and stared at the ceiling tiles. Eleven long and seven wide. Two primes, absolutely perfect. And, of course, added together they made eighteen, a multiple of three. What would I say if I were still taking my meds?

"Did I write that?" She asked. Of course, I did! It is the way of things. "It sounds odd to me."

"Don't you recognize it?" Dr. Schnell asked. He scribbled some notes in his book and looked at her over the top of his glasses.

"No sir." She ignored the urge to shake her head vehemently while answering. That would be a clear indicator I am free again. Am I getting the midwestern accent right?

Dr. Schnell smiled. It was clinical and clean, plastic with no emotion behind it. Only the intent to calm the patient while he continued his evaluation. He licked his thumb and forefinger, then turned the page to his notebook.

"How about this next part?" He said as he adjusted his glasses to read again.

Earth, Sea and Sky

Unlearn your understanding of the four elements taught to you in modern schools. Earth, wind, fire and water certainly all exist, but they do not make up all things in the universe. What they have come to be recognized as were born in the belly of creation, their meaning changed as mankind's understanding evolved.

Remember, three is the sacred number which grows from the one and the two. One is the fire of creation, the base of all things. That fire is at the center of all we are and all we know. It is the very spark of life. From this foundation grew the world tree.

The world tree is the other first recognized by the sacred fire. Its roots are fed by the fire and it grows to all realms, in all times. The world tree brought forth the three realms in which all life is held, the Earth, Sea and Sky.

The Earth is the world you know. Filled with ever evolving life and reaching out as far as the senses can perceive it. It is more than the planet on which you stand, it is the very dimension in which that planet exists. The planet was simply named after the realm by the first men, as they understood the nature of all existence.

The Sea lies just beyond the Earth. Like the oceans to land on our planet the Sea is always one tiny step from the shore. The great veil separates Earth and Sea, but those who know how and when can travel between them. The Sea is the birthplace of magic and the realm of creatures great and small. Magic spills over from Sea to Earth like tides washing up to the shore.

Surrounding it all is the Sky. Just as the air we breathe provides us with oxygen, so too does the Sky stoke the sacred fire of creation to provide for Earth and Sea. This is the place of gods and goddesses, those forces constantly circling Earth and Sea to impact all things. The Sky dances around Earth and Sea like children around a May pole, ever weaving the energies of creation and altering the destiny of life.

"Do you recognize that?" He asked.

"No sir." She lied. Yes! I will always recognize truth when I hear it. "Sounds a little, coo coo, if you ask me." She made a twirling motion with a finger next to her temple.

"Are you saying you think you are crazy?" Dr. Schnell sat forward in his seat, slightly.

"Not me." Melanie said. "But the whackadoodle who wrote that should be put up here with us!"

"Melanie, you wrote this." Dr. Schnell said.

"Oh, did I?" She asked with a perplexed look. "I don't remember that. I guess I am in the right place then." Her last sentence had the slightest lilt. The doctor didn't seem to notice.

"If you will, Melanie, I would like you to hear one more entry." The doctor turned the page and read, not waiting for permission.

The Veil

A thin mystical membrane separates Earth and Sea. As the mystical forces and creatures of the Sea cross over to Earth they bring with them magic itself. Religion, legend, folklore and myths of old were inspired by mankind's perception of these forces at work on Earth. This thin membrane is called the veil.

The veil varies in thickness and intensity depending upon a variety of factors. Some places around the world have become sacred for the ease of passage from Earth to Sea and back. This is also true for some seasons and some specific dates. These have evolved into holidays, in many cases. There are also specific plants and animals whose aura and perception easily pierce the veil. Mystical creatures have been known to travel from the Sea to Earth during the first light of day in the small area beneath the branches of a Hawthorn tree. Cats can see clearly through the veil at all times and have therefore become companions to many Earthly magical practitioners.

The most prolific points of access from Earth to Sea and back, for those who know how to cross, are called Moon Paths. When the moon crosses between our world and the sun its shadow pulls a tear in the veil. This tear eventually heals itself, but for 81 years the veil is thin enough to pass through freely in both directions provided certain circumstances hold true. This has had enormous impact on folklore in our world.

A Moon Path is only created during a total solar eclipse, and only where the moon's shadow was absolute. The duration is another example of the sacred three. Three, multiplied by three a total of three times gives 81. All things return to three.

"Any thoughts, Melanie." Dr. Schnell asked.

Melanie furrowed her brow as if contemplating. She bounced a finger in the air and incorrectly mouthed some of what he had read. *My first thought is that it proves my point you read me three parts of my own journal, boyo!* She smiled.

"I got a little lost in there, sir." She said. "Did the author say you could travel to another place if you were under a Hawthorn tree at sunrise?"

"Yes." He said abruptly. "And Melanie, you are the author."

"If I didn't trust you so much Dr. Schnell, I would call you a liar." She smiled. "I couldn't even follow all of that. I am surprised to hear I wrote it."

"So, I want to be clear." Dr. Schnell put on a very serious face. "None of these passages made you feel anxious in any way?"

She shook her head.

"They don't make you worry about goblins and elves coming to get us?" He continued.

She snorted and shook her head again.

Dr. Schnell closed his notebook and sat back. Relaxation washed over him and he began to straighten his files and tidy up the desk. He packed everything into a briefcase and stood. A genuine smile took his face as he offered a hand to help Melanie rise from her seat.

"After your episode right before the eclipse last month, some were worried you would be on the verge of panic." He said.

"I bet." Melanie laughed as genuinely as she knew how. "I'm terribly sorry about that. I don't know what came over me, sir." *Yes, I do! It was a full eclipse that cut a Moon Path right across the country. It's been a fecking month, all manner of beast is like to be walking through. And that's the least of it! We're, all of us, in fecking danger!*

"I understand, Melanie." Dr. Schnell put his hand on her shoulder. "Sometimes we all have a bad day. I'm just glad you pulled through it all so nicely. I am very proud of you."

"Thank you, sir." She said.

Dr. Schnell straightened his jacket, took his briefcase from the table, and turned for the door.

"You have a relaxing weekend, doctor's orders." He laughed. "Today was the last day of summer. Can you believe how fast it flew by?"

"Is it now?" Melanie said while laughing at his attempt to be funny. "What's the word for that? Sol-something?"

"Solstice." Dr. Schnell said smugly. "Ah, yes. Solstice." Melanie smiled.

"What the fuck kinda name is Yochanan?" asked Todd louder than necessary. Cursing was still a pretty new expression for him, so he was careful to enunciate the word very clearly. So much so it sounded misplaced among the gentle Midwestern slur flowing beneath the rest of his words.

"Shut up, Todd!" Eric shouted. He hated when other boys wanted to join their Saturday quests. Todd would always try to show off for them like he was auditioning for a part in their play. And so far, none had ever worked out. Always too much posturing and not enough commitment to their role.

"My name's Eric you big jerk. Everyone knows it." He said.

"Bull shit!" Todd hit the T extra hard to make sure no one mistook it for any other word. "If your name is Eric why does your mom call you Yoyo?" He punctuated his question with a harsh laugh and mocking points at Eric. He looked back to the two new boys for acceptance.

"I think it's a pretty badass name." said Mike. He was the tallest of the new boys and a 7th grader, so he knew way more about cool than any of them. "Can I call you Yoyo?" he asked in earnest.

Eric looked at the others uneasily, not sure how to answer. He couldn't tell whether Mike was being serious or if this was a subtler mockery.

Mike's little brother nodded in agreement as he pushed glasses back in place up the bridge of his nose. His name was also Tod but in the neighborhood they called him Single D to avoid confusion. Todd proper, with two Ds, looked at the brothers dumbfounded. Eric guessed from Todd's confusion Mike's question wasn't sarcasm.

"Um, yeah, I guess so." he said.

"Yochanan comes from the Hebrew language and means 'God is Gracious', which is quite unique and outstanding in my opinion." Single D always used twenty words when two would do. If he ever spoke at all, that is. Most of the time he stood by quietly and nodded in support of his brother. Sometimes he would even add a gesture with his nod.

"It's cool." said Mike. Single D nodded to indicate the affirmative while pointing at his brother with a thumb.

"Fucking A!" Todd hadn't heard his own voice for a while, nor had he cursed. Never one to let too much time pass between either he thought he would rejoin the pack and kill three birds with one phrase. He was, of course, very careful to correctly and distinctly pronounce every syllable to make certain he was understood.

Eric stood a little straighter knowing he had the favor of the new boys. Maybe letting them join the quest this week wouldn't be so bad. He looked at Todd with an expression of "What do you think?" and gave a shrug. Todd replied with a nod of "Yeah, they're cool." Which he hoped wasn't so enthusiastic it made him look over eager.

"So, we're gonna go get our gear and meet back at the angel." Eric scratched the back of his head and looked at his feet. "You guys wanna quest with us today?"

"Yeah man." said Mike. Single D nodded in agreement, giving his glasses another push up his nose while Mike continued. "What professions are you guys?"

"I'm a rage fueled mother fucking Barbarian, man." Todd beamed. "And Yoyo is an expert tracker. He knows the woods better'n anyone."

"I'm a Ranger." Eric clarified. "Shit yes!" said Todd.

"How about you guys?" Eric asked. He hoped that at least one of them used magic. A healer would be ideal. That and maybe another fighter of some sort. His train of thought turned full wish list for a moment before Eric realized he didn't really care as long as the new members were into their roles. Saturday quest was about the adventure and the role play. If it was just going to be a couple dudes hanging out while he and Todd were questing the whole day would lose all its magic.

"I'm a Paladin and Single D is a magic user." Mike stood as tall as he could. Single D nodded with a grin and took a breath as if about to speak. Then shrugged and nodded some more.

Eric smiled broadly. They couldn't be a better fit for the party. A fighting healer and someone who could cast. What a great balance they had. This would be the best Saturday quest yet!

"So then, the angel at 1:30?" asked Eric. "Enough time to gear up and have some lunch?"

"Sounds good." said Mike as Single D nodded.

"Fucking A right it does!" Todd got in his last curse before lunch and the boys disbanded until 1:30.

Eric ran in the door, past his mother, and into his room with a practiced grace. He waved and made the shape of a heart with his hands as he passed her. She smiled and blew him a kiss. Still smiling as he closed the door to his room, he took a deep breath in preparation.

The room was meticulously clean for a boy Eric's age. There was an order and structure to his space that gave him comfort. Not in an obsessive or compulsive way, rather, as a balance to the chaotic structure of the outside world. Nature was not to be tamed, but the den was.

He kicked his sneakers into their corner and pulled his boots from beneath his bed. Jeans were already a part of his uniform so there was no need to change them. He pulled a green hooded sweat shirt on over his Star Wars t-shirt and fixed the sleeves the way he liked them, with three cuff rolls on the right arm and four on the left.

From his wall he took down the Bear recurved bow his father got him for his 12th birthday. He had petitioned his parents, at length, to let him take actual arrows on quests but he was denied repeatedly. Eric didn't let it fester into an argument or a sore spot. The bow was enough to help him be in character.

For finishing touches he threw his khaki messenger bag over his head and shoulder to hang on his left side.

As he ran into the kitchen to grab a couple sandwiches for his bag his mother made it a point to get eye contact. When she was sure he was watching she spoke to him using American Sign Language.

"You and your friends are going on your Saturday quest?" she signed. "Yes ma'am." He said while nodding.

"Be safe and keep dry this time, please." She signed.

Eric was secretly very happy his mother spoke using sign. She never seemed to harp on him like other boys' mothers. There was a gleam in her eye and smile on her face with every word. It gave him a very clear sign of her love for him.

"I will mom." He signed.

She liked that Eric spent time outside actually playing instead of cooped up with some video game. So many boys his age were wrapped up with their Xbox or smart phone and hardly saw the light of day. Eric played games like that some, but he mostly preferred the outdoors. It warmed her heart.

"You have your watch?" She asked. After he nodded, pointing to his bag, she continued to sign. "And you will be home by 5:00, in time for dinner, right?"

Eric nodded again and gave his mother a loving hug. She dropped a chocolate bar into his messenger bag when he wasn't looking and waved as he hopped out the door. With fluid agility he bounded around a gate to the back yard and over some railroad ties used for landscaping. He landed with a spectacular pose next to his dog Boomer.

Boomer was a chocolate brown labradoodle. A bumbling ball of hyperactive, slobbering and loyal energy so devoted to Eric he could barely contain himself. Eric knelt down to say hi with scratches and unhooked Boomer's leash. It was entirely possible Boomer liked Saturday quest more than any of the boys did.

Once unhooked he frolicked around Eric with glee. Never moving more than ten or twelve feet away from him before coming back and checking in. He vigilantly watched for squirrels, villains, monsters and other dogs, not necessarily in that order.

Eric's yard was bordered by a fence with a thin tree line in the back. On the other side was a five-acre field at the front of a cemetery. The field routinely flooded so no plots were sold here. Instead it was well groomed and served to make the cemetery look more open and inviting. Behind the field was a small hill rising about 20 feet up to a plateau on which plots were laid out.

Eric and Boomer sprinted across the field and up the hill into the cemetery. They followed the fence line which continued from behind Eric's house on up the hill. The thin tree line slowly expanded to a finger of woods about 50 yards across for a quarter mile. There the fence ended with the property line of the last house on Eric's cul-de-sac. The cemetery bordered bare woods from this point on to the back.

Just beyond the end of the fence was a beautiful headstone carved in the shape of an angel. It stood, looking at the heavens, with its arms raised up in praise and its wings spread majestically. As it came into view Eric noticed Mike and Single D had already arrived. Todd wasn't there yet so Eric decided to save his breath and stop running.

Eric was in awe. Mike was actually wearing armor. His shins and knees were covered in baseball shin guards painted silver over heavy boots and blue jeans. His thighs and mid-section were covered with hockey leg guards customized to allow for movement and also painted silver. Small shoulder pads covered his chest and shoulders painted the same silver. Over it all he wore a tabard, belted at the waist and a red cloak attached to his chest in front using the laces of the shoulder pads. In his right hand, point in the ground, was a large wooden sword fashioned in the style of a bastard sword and on his left arm was a trash can lid made into a shield.

It was amazing.

Single D was decked out in character too. He wore layers of red and maroon robes with a black and maroon cloak. Across one shoulder he carried a red leather bag shaped like a giant book. It was adorned with feathers and had various sigils painted on it. Around his neck was a pendant with a red stone in the center. His hood was drawn up over his head and he leaned on a staff made from the heavy handle of a mop.

Single D noticed Eric approaching and tapped his brother's shoulder with a nod to let him know. Mike turned slowly, head held high and shoulders back. He smiled at Eric with approval as he and his hound approached the brothers.

"Well met, Ranger." Mike said. "Who is your companion?"

"Hail Paladin. Mage." Eric gave a slight bow of respect to Mike and nodded to Single D. "He is called Boomer. My longtime friend and partner in protection of these woods."

Single D nodded with a smile before dropping to one knee to meet and greet Boomer. Boomer took the queue and happily approached the hooded boy. Tod gave copious scratches behind the ears while Boomer wagged his body and kissed the boy a wet greeting. He stood with a giggle and gave Eric a thumbs up and a smile.

"What's up bitches!" Todd hopped a fence to join the group. "Are you fuckers ready to start mother fucking Saturday quest?"

Single D shook his head.

"Todd, while I appreciate the correct pronunciation of your curse words, I would like to point out that none of us are impressed by either your ability to say them or the carelessness with which they flow from your mouth." Single D said. "Yeah man, uncool." Mike followed.

Eric just smiled to himself. These guys just might work out after all. They were a good fit for the party, they didn't take any of Todd's braggadocios crap and they were entirely immersed in their characters.

Sadly, Todd probably wouldn't change his vocabulary based on their observations. It was more likely he would dismiss it entirely.

"What-fucking-ever, man." Todd said. "I'm cool as shit, man."

After the group eye roll at Todd's proclamation the new members sized up his gear. He carried a reclaimed tree branch he had stripped the bark from. The ends were crudely cut and beaten into the shape of a club. He had wrapped dark leather straps around the handle area for grip and effect.

He wore leather boots with brown fur cuffs just below his knees. His cutoff jean shorts were well hidden beneath a tan leather apron fashioned into a long loin cloth gathered with a thick brown leather belt. None of the tones matched, which gave a natural and worn feel to it all.

On his upper body he wore an old fox fur coat with the arms cut off and buttons removed. His mother made him wear a shirt beneath it so he chose one as close to flesh colored as he could find. Topping everything off was a coon skin cap that would make Davey Crocket proud.

"Nice gear though, dude." Mike said. Single D nodded enthusiastically and fixed his glasses.

"Let's head out then." Eric said. "Boomer and I will take point."

He ran out ahead of the other boys a few paces, careful to stay in earshot. Boomer inspected headstones and benches near them and kept an eye toward the woods. Mike held up his shield and nodded his head to the rear of the line. He stepped behind Single D and gestured for Todd to take the position behind Eric in line. Todd nodded with a barbaric grunt and stepped in front of the diminutive magic user. The party moved out to follow the white rocked cemetery road to the rear where fewer plots were in use.

At the very back of the cemetery the manicured grounds extended twenty yards beyond the road and then abruptly turned into untended prairie. Two trails led off at opposite angles through the tall grass. The left was in the direction of train tracks a couple hundred yards to the southwest and the right led northwest to a corner of woods poking into the prairie. They took the right path.

At the edge of the woods there was a very slight incline to the trees. A few quick steps up and they were into the canopy. In the woods the trail was just wide enough for one. No one maintained the trail but it was well worn. Local kids and some smaller woodland creatures used it regularly. It was early September and summer still hung in the air but the bugs were starting to thin. Everything was beautiful and green, no sign of the approaching autumn. This was Eric's favorite time of year to quest. It wasn't sweltering like the summer. Plant life was mature and lush, unlike the youthful budding of spring. And the turn to fall was still a couple weeks away.

Animals frequented these woods regularly. The land was owned by the cemetery all the way back to a healthy creek and hunting was banned. On the west side of the creek was a nature preserve maintained by the county and some privately-owned land where hunting was also discouraged. All told there were nearly 250 acres of woodland free of hunters. Animals flocked here as a result.

About 80 yards in on the trail the woods thinned slightly. The party neared the top of a hill the boys called junction knob. From here there were two paths down the hill that led to different sides of a large clearing below. Five larger trails and half a dozen smaller ones led from the clearing to different corners of the woods. Sometimes the older kids would be here smoking pot but today they were absent. They must have been getting high in someone's basement instead.

Eric stopped with a gasp and held up a single fist to silently signal the group to stop.

"I found a track." He said excitedly, belaying the need for a silent signal. "Come look, it is wicked cool."

The other boys crowded together to view what turned out to be two sets of tracks. The older of the pair were canine, likely that a fox or a small dog. The newer set looked like deer tracks, but something wasn't quite right. They were huge.

"Holy shit!" This time it was Eric who swore. "These are deer tracks, but they are way too big. I've seen tracks left by a big buck with my dad. Like, a ten pointer, and they were only about this big."

He held up his hands between three and four inches apart. Eyes wide he moved them down to the tracks to show that they were easily twice that size. The tracks didn't show the telltale zig zag of a deer in flight, rather, they were evenly spaced indicating a slow and steady gate.

"And it's just weird that they are actually following the fox." Eric didn't really know if the canine tracks were that of a fox, but he was certain his character would.

"We should fucking investigate." Todd said with the most grizzled voice he could muster.

"Agreed." said Mike with a slight accent. "If this is some unnatural creature it could put travelers in danger. We mustn't allow that." Single D nodded with a grim expression.

The four followed the odd tracks further north toward the creek. Eric and Boomer stayed out front and kept an eye on their surroundings as they identified sign for the trail. It was quite easy with the double sized deer tracks. Boomer was the first to notice the smell.

He shot off into the woods barking protectively. Eric scrunched his nose when the smell hit him. It was something dead. He started to follow Boomer but stopped when he lost sight of him. He looked back at the others and held up his fist to hold. They complied with silent nods and Eric turned and rushed off into the thick.

Todd neared the point where Eric left the trail and looked in the direction the Ranger and his dog had run. The only sound were the steps of Mike and Single D as they slowly caught up to him. There were no longer birds calling. Even the wind seemed quiet. The three squinted, trying to make out any movement of their friends. Single D fixed his gaze in the distance and was about to speak.

"You guys!" Eric screamed from deeper in the woods. "Come quick, this is messed up!"

There was almost panic in his voice. Mike started toward Eric full speed with no hesitation at all. Single D looked at Todd, then followed. Todd gripped his club and ran beside Single D. His head was on a swivel, nothing would escape his notice while he protected the mage. Single D was secretly impressed.

Mike was the first to catch up to Eric and Boomer. Eric was looking down a small hill at Boomer as Mike stepped beside him. The curly brown tail wagged the dog as he sniffed the grounds around something Mike couldn't quite make out. He craned his neck for a better view as the other boys arrived. When he realized what he was looking at his eyes went wide. The animal carcass was ravaged. Torn apart by claws, bites, or something wild.

"Is?" Mike stammered. "Is that a?" he stopped to wretch, holding back the sick as the smell finally hit him too. "Is that a coyote?"

"No fucking way!" said Todd as he and Single D caught up.

"I find that difficult to believe as a coyote is both larger, and arguably more fierce and formidable than either a red or gray fox. It is unlikely there are any predators that would kill one in this part of the state other than man." Single D said.

"It's a coyote, Tod." Mike said.

Single D gasped at his brother's use of his given name. He immediately scanned their surroundings and it finally occurred to him that no birds were singing. Eric noticed the brothers' escalated level of worry and looked at Todd for a quick read. There were no curse words, no chest puffing, no club waving. Todd was scared, and it had manifested in absolute still silence for him.

"We need to investigate more." Eric said. "See if we can figure out who or what did this."

Mike gave a slow sigh of resolve and stood tall. He gripped his sword and adjusted his shield. He surveyed the area with a squint and a grim expression. Single D leaned his staff against a tree and pulled a heavy- duty wrist rocket slingshot from his book bag. He secured it to his arm ang pulled out a bag of marbles with his free hand.

"Are you guys fucking nuts?!?" Todd screamed. His voice nearly squeaked and his normally careful annunciation evaporated. "Something fucking killed a coyote in our fucking woods and you want to fucking investigate?"

Eric didn't stick around for the debate, he went down to the carcass and studied it. The first thing he noticed was that the longer lacerations weren't claw marks like they had originally thought. They were wider and shallower gashes than a claw would make. Instead of four parallel cuts for each strike there were two. They almost looked like the same hooves that made those giant prints could have done this.

That didn't sync up with the other wounds though. There was bite damage all over the coyote. Not bites like any large cat or wolf would make though. Some weird hybrid bites that had deep cutting severs from front teeth in combination with tears and rips from large lower teeth like that of a boar. All the bites were from above the coyote indicating a predator that was at least five feet tall, possibly taller.

"Um, guys." Eric turned and made a silent sign to Boomer who came to his side immediately. "I think Todd is right, we should leave. I don't know what did this but whatever it was it was…"

Eric was cut off by the terrified scream of Todd who backed into Mike and Single D. Tod and Todd alike tumbled down the hill to stop at Eric's feet. Mike was knocked off balance and tried to keep his feet as he slid down toward the other boys. He held up his shield defensively and readied his sword for what Todd had seen. No one could have guessed what that was.

Above them on the ridge was an enormous beast that resembled a stag but with serious differences. The thing was over six feet tall and built more like a heavy war horse than a lithe and agile forest creature. Its antlers were an ivory white nearly five inches in diameter at their base and spreading up to a majestic, and bloody, sixteen points.

Its coat was black along the spine, not that the boys could see its spine, and slowly turned auburn and then scarlet as it met the ground. Large teeth framed the beast's sneering mouth. Long curving chisels from the top looped over the lower jaw like a devil beaver. Four tusks pushed up, two on each side of its snout, just outside them. Razor sharp and stained with blood.

It huffed aggressively at the boys as it stepped to the hill's edge, eyes locked on Mike's shield. It tested the ground at the crest and backed, agitated, from the loose dirt. It rose into an angry rear and made a noise that was part scream and part howl. That's when the boys saw that its tail was on fire. No, it was fire.

"OH MY FUCKING GOD, WHAT THE FUCK IS THAT?!?" screamed Todd.

"Don't use the lord's name in vain dick hole." Mike scolded while keeping his eyes on the beast and his shield up.

Single D put a marble in the sling of the wrist rocket and pulled to aim. Todd raised his club and stepped beside Mike, urine running down his leg. The beast came down from its rear with a thud and scraped at the loose dirt in front of it. Eric made a gesture to send Boomer back home, but the pooch was looking up. Not at the beast though, he was looking behind Eric and into the branches above.

The little mage let his glass bullet fly as Eric turned to look up. The marble shattered on the ridge above the beast's right eye and made him recoil. Mike raised the point of his sword toward the stag in case it charged downhill and Eric caught sight of what had Boomer's attention. It was a great horned owl swooping toward them. It was strange.

There were plenty of raptors in this part of Illinois. Hawks and kites, maybe even an eagle now and then. But not a great horned owl. Maybe if one escaped from a zoo or something, but this one didn't. Owls like this one wouldn't fly straight at humans and most certainly wouldn't fly at a monster like the demon stag. But none of that was the strange part. What was strange was that it was carrying three arrows in its talons.

The beast was bleeding now above its eye. Bleeding and angry. Any caution it had about its footing for a charge had now vanished. It reared again and lowered its head toward the furry urine scented creature and charged. Todd held his ground, screaming, and swung his club down toward the beast's lowered head. Mike managed to get his shield in front of the beast's antlers to protect Todd as his club came down hard on its head. It glanced off Mike's shield and shook its head dizzily as it stumbled to their right.

The owl dropped the three arrows at Eric's feet and landed between the beast and the boys. Single D let another marble fly, this time striking the beast directly in the eye. It let loose another scream and charged the tiny mage. Eric fumbled to get an arrow nocked and had enough time to get off one shot that stuck in the monster's face but did not drop him. Boomer jumped in front of Single D, but he wouldn't stand a chance. Eric thought all was lost but then the

volume of crazy on this day went all the way up to eleven.

The owl transformed into a grizzly bear in less time than it would take to say, "turn me into a bear." The grizzly stepped in front of the charge and soaked the antler damage meant for Single D. With a determined grunt and no shortage of anger it gashed both sides of the monster's neck. Although surrounded by large and dense muscles, the claws found both the carotid artery and jugular vein. It then laid on the monster's head until it bleed out.

"What the fuck is happening?" Todd was in tears now as the adrenaline started to fade.

Mike got to his feet and stepped between the bear and his brother. Eric knelt to check on Single D who had been knocked to the ground with Boomer in the fray. He was weeping silently and staring at the dead monster beneath the bear. Boomer licked the tears from his face trying to assure him all was well. Eric, in shock, stared at the second arrow he had picked up. He looked up at the bear, trying to piece it all together.

"It's a druid." he said. "That's the only explanation." "Aye." Mike said as Single D nodded through tears. "What fucking ever." Todd wept.

The bear slowly pulled itself from the monster's antlers. It let out grunt part sigh and part growl and sat back heavily onto its haunches. Pawing at the puncture wounds on its belly it cocked its head to the side like a confused dog and looked at the Ranger. Slowly, as all four boys stared in amazement, the animal turned from grizzly to human. A naked, bleeding, human woman. Mike removed his cloak and draped it over her shoulders to modestly cover her exposed lady parts.

"Níl tú ach buachaillí beaga!" The lady scolded. She waved a finger at the boys sternly. "Is dúr leis an óige, buachaillí beaga bídeacha." She held up her thumb and fore finger in a manner to indicate something small.

The boys stared at her in shock. Boomer was the only one paying any attention to the felled demon stag now. He sniffed and pawed at it, not noticing the woman at all. Single D pushed his way to the front of the group and cleared his throat.

"Begging your pardon, ma'am, but we do not speak Irish. I hope that you also understand English as I would like to extend our thanks to you for stopping that unnatural beast from shortening our lives." He smiled and extended his right hand while his left pushed his glasses back home on his nose.

"Yeah, thanks." Mike said.

"Not so stupid that ye don't know Irish when ye hear it though." She said with a smile. Her accent was so thick the boys had to concentrate to understand her. "Ye're welcome lads."

"You were a fucking bear!" Todd screamed. "How the fuck?"

"Aye, I was a fecking bear." She smiled as she stood. "And ye are fortunate I was." Her scolding tone returned with a face to match. "A Totanaki is no beast for wee boys t'be fightin'!"

She brushed the cloak to make sure she was covered and knelt to the stag's head. She grabbed the arrow protruding from the meat of its face and plucked it out with a twist. As she turned, Eric saw that the punctures on her stomach were closed and seemed to have healed some. She noticed his gaze and pulled the cloak to cover her skin.

"I'll be fine, wee Ranger. When I shift it heals me some." She held the arrow out to him. "Me brudder's a Ranger, lad. Ye'll need these arrows if 'n ye want to protect yer mates."

Eric took the arrow with a silent smile. He studied the three of them closer now the impending peril had passed. They were ash wood stained a sage green color. The fletching was owl feathers bound with fine cotton thread. Each shaft had a series of hand carved runes. Eric made note to look up their meanings later. He was most impressed with the arrow heads. Each was made of stone, two red jasper and one forest agate. He ran his thumb along one's edge and found it razor sharp, slicing him with barely any pressure.

"Careful lad, those are my handy work. Very sharp." She took his hand gently and inspected the cut. Keeping his hand in hers she knelt and pinched some dirt with her free hand. She closed her eyes and lifted her chin. The air seemed to follow her queue and blew her hair back as she took a deep breath. She then rubbed the soil into his cut. He watched in awestruck shock as she brushed the dirt away from the perfectly healed thumb.

"Wait, no!" Todd was having a hard time keeping it together. "You are a real fucking druid?" Tears rolled down his face and his breathing quickened. His gaze darted from the stag, to the woman, to the arrows and to Eric's thumb. He was on the verge of a panic attack when Mike put a hand on Todd's shoulder.

"Todd, it's OK. We're here and you are safe." Mikes words were calm and peaceful. Todd looked at Mike's eyes and began to calm. His breathing slowed and with it, his mind. The warmth of Mike's touch spread through his body until he was fully relaxed.

"I'm good man." Todd said. "Thanks Mike. I'm good."

Eric stowed the arrows in his messenger bag and turned his attention back to the woman. She was scratching Boomer behind the ears while he kissed her face. Who was she? Where did she come from? Were there more druids? Her brother is a Ranger. What does that mean?

"Um, miss?" Eric asked. "I have some questions. If I may."

"Of course, wee man." She said. "We can talk while I walk you boys back out of the woods."

"Wait, no." Mike said. "If there are more of these beasts out here we need to stop them."

"I like yer pluck, lad." The lady stood and approached Mike as she spoke. "Ye're all lucky, this Totanaki was a young one."

"Wait, young?" Eric asked. "But it has sixteen points."

"Aye Ranger. Young." She smiled. "Beasts of the Sea and Sky don't behave like they do here on the Earth."

"Sea and Sky?" Single D seemed confused. "This creature has

neither gills nor wings, ma'am."

"Melanie." She said. "Please call me Melanie, lad. Or Mel. Ma'am is what ye call yer mum. I dinna mean sea like in the water, lad. It's a mystic Sea."

She saw confusion on all the boys faces. Knowing she had their attention she began to walk toward the cemetery as she explained. The boys followed without question, mesmerized by her story like she was the Pied Piper leading them from Hamelin.

"There are three realms of this life, lads. Three is an important number, remember it. Recognize it. All things, good and bad, come in threes. Like the Totanaki, back there. It is the third I have slain in these woods."

"What do you do with them." Eric asked.

"I ask the ground to take them. We are old mates, the ground and me." She said.

"Three planes." Mike said.

"Aye, lad." Melanie came back to her topic. "They are the Earth, Sea and Sky.

They all intersect at the sacred fire and spread out to the realms of all life. Human, beast, plant, stone and spirit all dwell on Earth, Sea and Sky.

The sacred fire, Brighid's grace, unites us all.

The Earth is home of humans, you and me, as well as the plants and animals 'round the world. It's the common world where most of us spend our entire lives. Each playin' our part in the great braiding of things. Weaving together the knotwork of our stories and purpose best we know how.

Then there's the Sea, the wild waste that lies outside our common land. It's just behind the veil and teaming with life, different from us. It's the place of the Otherworld Isles, the home of the Sidhe heroes and the land of the young. If 'n ye know where to look you can travel to and fro twixt Earth and Sea.

And last but greatest of the realms is the Sky where Light and Shadow are born. It's the place of the Shining Ones. It soars above the Earth and Sea just as the sight of the Gods and Goddesses watches us all. It turns, ever waxing and waning like our moon, dancing with stars like a May pole 'round us always.

And in the midst of all these worlds is found the Sacred Grove united by Brighid. The place of flowing together where she keeps the Sacred Fire burning by the Well of Wisdom beneath the World Tree."

As Melanie finished her story the six of them emerged from the woods where the boys had entered. No longer shaded by the canopy, light bounded from her strawberry blonde hair and ice blue eyes. The boys stood, slack jawed, in awe of both she and her story. Boomer leaned heavily against her leg, his version of a hug.

"Now, off with ye wee lads." She made a shooing motion toward their homes. "Yer parents'll be worried after ye and I have more work to do."

"But we can help," Eric pleaded.

"Yeah," Mike said while Single D nodded in unison. "It's our duty."

Todd just stared longingly at Melanie. Since experiencing the Paladin's calming influence after their battle the Barbarian was living less loudly. He sighed as she made eye contact with him.

"Aye, and ye will," she said. A serious look on her brow. She knelt and brought the boys in closely for a huddle. "I need the four of you, and Boomer, to patrol these woods after today."

All four stood as tall and proud as they could.

"What if we find something?" Eric asked. "Like more Totanaki tracks, or something worse?"

"I'm glad ye asked, wee Ranger." Melanie said. She cupped her hand behind Eric's ear and pulled a Blue Lace Agate from her palm as if it had been back there all along. "Speak into this stone and leave it by a Hawthorn tree just before sunrise, and I'll hear what ye said to it."

The boys made sounds of awe and crowded Eric for a closer look at the stone. Melanie stood back up and walked up the slight incline to the trail's mouth at the wood line.

"If 'n ye need me, lads, I'll come runnin'."

With a wink and a smile she pulled her hands under Mike's cloak, to her sides. Her beautiful face shifted into the great horned owl they had seen earlier. She sloughed off the cloak and beat her wings to take flight. A quick circle and a mighty screech later and she was gone. Back into the woods where they found her.

"You guys." Todd said. "Melanie is a really for real Druid." He smiled. "You didn't curse." Single D said as he pushed his glasses back into place. He smiled with approval as Mike picked up his cloak and the five began their trip back to hearth and home.

Excerpt from Life in Lemon Creek
By Kathy Jimerson

That night, after a microwaved frozen dinner, which he barely touched, Daniel sat alone in the family room of his brand new, oversized home.

A football game was playing on the enormous, wall-mounted plasma TV, but Daniel couldn't seem to concentrate on it. The vision of Marta's slender fingers pushing back that stray lock of hair kept popping up between Daniel and the fifty-yard line.

Daniel had never been one much for introspection. He was a man who saw a situation and acted on it. If it didn't work out, he rarely regretted anything--not because he couldn't recognize his mistakes, but because what was done was done.

But tonight he was questioning himself. He wondered if this love he felt for Marta was really more of an obsession. If not, why was he fixated on that one little habitual gesture of hers. Why did that image keep interrupting his football game? He'd never had this trouble before. Not with Lucy. Certainly not with Beth. These were his only two points of reference, because contrary to certain people's beliefs, there had never been any other women in his life. He and Beth had been high school sweethearts who had simply fallen into marriage right after college because it seemed the thing to do. As for Lucy, he had loved her, but was it possible that you think you've found the real thing until the real real thing comes along? For that matter, was there any such thing as the real thing?

Or, alternatively, was he nothing more than a plain old lech-- an old guy lusting after a fresh young thing? He didn't feel like a lech. He couldn't be because when he thought about Marta, he didn't think about sex that much. Okay, that was a lie. He might be middle-aged, but he wasn't dead. He was a man, and Marta was a beautiful woman. Yes, he thought about making love to her--a lot. But he also thought about the surprising things she said all the time, about the way she challenged him and had done from the first moment they met, about her loyalty to Lucy and anyone else she cared about, about how she loved Joshua. And, after all, Star Wars was her favorite movie.

Maybe he was just having a midlife crisis. Should he just buy a red sports car and leave poor Marta alone?

Maybe he was simply on the rebound from Lucy. But no. He dismissed that notion at once. Marta was not a rebound kind of girl.

She was the sort you rebounded from.

The only thing he was sure of was that he had never felt this way before.

He suddenly realized he'd been pacing the floor. He didn't like all this self-analysis. He was unaccustomed to it, and it was exhausting.

With a sigh of frustration, he picked up the phone. There was only one thing to do. Call the one person in the world who would know the answers to all his questions.

"Lucy?" he said when she answered. "Hi, Daniel. What's up?"

"I need you to answer the following question." "Okaaay," she said tentatively.

"Would you say I am either A, a lecherous old man; B, an obsessive personality; or C, going through a midlife crisis?"

"Are those my only choices?" "Yes."

"I assume this has to do with Marta." "Just answer the question."

Lucy hesitated. For a brief moment she considered telling him about Marta's conversation with James Lee. But it seemed like a betrayal of a confidence, even though nobody involved had exacted any vow of secrecy.

"Okay," she said. "None of the above." "Aha! I knew it!"

"Please, Daniel, don't take this as approval of…" "Lucy?" Daniel interrupted.

"Yes?"

"Remember the other night you said I don't know the meaning of love? Well, maybe I didn't know because I hadn't found it yet. Now don't get me wrong," he rushed to say. "I don't mean to take anything away from what we had, but I think you yourself would say it wasn't half what you feel for James Lee. Am I right?"

"Of course, you are, but…"

"No buts. You basically agreed with me and you can't take it back.

Thanks, Luce. I gotta go."

"Daniel! Wait! What are you going to do?" "I'm not sure. But something."

"Daniel, if you hurt Marta, I'll murder you."

"I won't. I promise. I'd rather cut off my right arm than hurt Marta.

Okay, hanging up now." "Daniel!"

"What?"

"Whatever happens, I do want the best for you. I really do." "Then wish me luck."

"Good luck...I think."

"Who was that?" asked James Lee, who walked in just as Lucy was hanging up the phone.

"Daniel."

"Oh? What's his problem now?"

"I'm not completely sure," said Lucy pensively. "Either...A, he's about to be deliriously happy; B, he's about to screw up royally; or C, he's about to become a murder victim."

"Huh?"

"Nothing, honey," said Lucy going into his arms where everything was safe and calm.

"I guess we should be rooting for option A,"

"You're too nice, James Lee--wanting Daniel to be happy despite your differences."

"Not when you consider the choices you gave me. Screwing up royally would probably involve Marta getting hurt, and surely anything is better than being a murder victim--especially since the murderer, I'm guessing, would be you, and Josh and I just can't do without you for twenty to life."

Lucy snuggled deeper into his embrace. "Is it wrong that I'm glad it's them and not us?"

"Probably," James Lee allowed. "But I couldn't agree more."

Excerpt from The Alien Who Looked Like Kang Ji Soo
Kathy Jimerson

On Wednesdays, Jasmine and her co-workers were in the habit of celebrating hump day with drinks and fattening foods at one of the many bars that lined Coastal Boulevard. Their favorite was a place called Snapper's Pub, which specialized in raw oysters, imported beers and deep-fried appetizers. Snapper's had a nice outdoor beer garden, but this day was cold and rainy. The usual group sat inside at a big table in the center of the room--Missy, Geneva, Robbie, Karen, Todd and Jasmine.

"You're awfully quiet, Jaz," said Karen. Her tone conveyed concern with just a touch, perhaps, of pity.

Jasmine made a visible effort to perk up. "Am I?" she said as brightly as she could. "It's not intentional." She smiled unconvincingly and took a sip of her martini.

"Leave Jaz alone," Geneva scolded.

While everyone else at the table, was under forty, Geneva was nearing retirement and had been with the bank for thirty years. This circumstance accorded her the unofficial, but undisputed, title of mother hen. She delicately selected a fried dill pickle from the giant appetizer sampler she had ordered for the table. "Grigsby was really on the warpath today, wasn't he? That man will be the death of me," she said, changing the subject.

"Grigsby," Todd groaned. "How did we get so lucky to have a boss like that?"

"He really sucks," Jasmine muttered almost inaudibly.

Missy, the intern, leaned over toward Jasmine. "Are you crying?"

Jasmine stood and gathered up her purse. She tossed a twenty onto the table. "Sorry, guys, I have to go. I just can't do this today." She paused just a moment while her friends bombarded her with questions and expressions of sympathy.

"What is it, Jaz?" Karen asked.

Jasmine's sniffles changed to outright sobs. "My snake is gone!" she blubbered as she turned and fled.

Robbie looked to Geneva for guidance. "Should we go after her...or what?"

"Just let her be," Geneva replied calmly. "Just let her cry it out. She'll be okay."

"Um...did she say her snake is gone?" Missy inquired.

"Yes," Geneva answered, stuffing a fried mushroom into her mouth. "What the hell," said Todd. "Jaz has a pet snake? I never heard her

mention it, and she definitely doesn't seem like the type." "It wasn't a pet," said Geneva.

"Okay, Gen, stop with the cryptic remarks," Karen demanded. "You seem to know all about this. Spill."

Geneva took a swig of her beer. "Well, okay. I don't think she'd mind if I told you. A few weeks ago, she went out to her car and there was a snake coiled up in her parking space at the condo. It was small like a garter snake or something. For some reason, she didn't think it looked poisonous. It wasn't in the way of her getting into the car, so she decided to let it be. She figured it would slither off somewhere, but when she got back it was still there. It had moved some—farther toward the front of the parking space. She still ignored it. After that, every time she came out to her car or arrived home, it was still there—in slightly different locations, but still there. After a while, she started looking for it, expecting to see it. One time it had moved to the other side of the—what do call that cement thingy in front of your car…"

"I don't know," said everyone in unison.

"I don't think they have a name," Todd declared.

"Of course, they have a name," Karen retorted. "Everything has a name. What do you think they do when they have to order more of them? Call up and ask for a hundred thingies?"

Geneva cleared her throat loudly. "That's not really important to my story."

"Sorry," said Todd. "Go on."

"Anyway, she didn't see it right away and found herself looking for it. She actually felt relieved when she found it behind the, you know, thingy. From then on, she developed a sort of attachment to it. She even contacted the condo management and asked them to tell the groundskeepers to be careful of it and not hurt it. She started to look on it as a sort of sign. Like if it was there, everything would be okay, you know? Still, she knew in her heart of hearts, the day would come when it would no longer be there. This went on for over a month. And then a few days ago when she got home from work, the snake was missing. She looked everywhere—all around the parking lot and all over the lawn. It was no use. For a while, she hoped it would come back. Maybe it was just off getting something to eat, but it never came back, and she finally accepted that it was never coming back."

"Well, that's a weird story," said Todd, chomping down on an enormous cheeseburger that the waitress had just delivered.

"So," Missy said, "if she thought the snake was a sign everything would be okay, its absence means everything is not okay. Right? And that's why she's so upset?"

"Partly that and, I think, partly she really felt attached to the snake.

After all, it is—or was—a living creature."

"But Jaz never even had a dog or a goldfish as far as I know," Robbie observed. "She never had any great feeling for animals."

"What can I tell you?" Geneva replied. "Things change. People change. Besides, Jasmine's going through some stuff right now. I'm sure that's part of it, too."

"She has seemed bummed for a while," Missy agreed.

"A long while. What's up with that?" Karen asked. "And how do you know so much about Jaz?" Although Karen didn't particularly want to be close to Jaz, she was a little jealous. She tended to be jealous of other people's friendships in general.

"I don't know exactly. We always seem to be in the lunchroom at the same time. She tells me stuff. I think I'm kind of a motherly figure to her. You know she and her own mom have issues. I'm so much older than all of you babies as you never fail to remind me," Geneva laughed. "Jaz is kind of an old soul I think."

"Old soul?" said Missy.

"Yeah. You know how she likes old movies and old music— things like that. I don't know. There's just something about her, don't you think?"

Missy shrugged and stabbed a mozzarella stick with her fork. "I guess so. I never thought about it."

"Anyway, she has not confided in me about whatever has been bothering her other than the snake situation. I can't help you there."

"Well, the whole thing is really odd," Karen said. "Jaz was always a bit of a flake, but I never thought she was actually nuts."

This comment was met with a protective chorus of, "She's not nuts!

She's not a flake!"

"But," Todd interrupted loudly, "I wonder if she knows snakes are phallic symbols."

"Oh, Todd," Geneva replied with a giggle. "I'm sure she does. Jaz was an English major."

An Excerpt from The Brothers Choi
By Kathy Jimerson

On the outskirts of Seoul, there's a stately house of pale pink brick with tall, white-trimmed windows. It sits amidst expansive, carefully tended lawns with sculpted hedges and flowering trees. At the back of the property, there's an orchard where apples, cherries and persimmons grow.

Behind the house, a flagstone terrace runs the length of the structure. There, a young boy sits at a glass-top table working at his studies. He sits upon two silk pillows which raise him up so that he can reach the tabletop, his little legs dangling below. His texts and workbooks are spread out before him. He scrunches up his forehead in concentration. Math comes easily to him, but he wants his work to be perfect. His name is Choi Jae Sung. He is seven years old.

A long driveway of gleaming white gravel leads to a garage that houses no fewer than six automobiles. An older boy, only sixteen months older to be sure, pokes his head around the corner of the garage, then quickly ducks back. He repeats this process several times as he clutches a giant soaker water gun in his small hands. He waits, calculating the perfect opportunity. When the time comes, he places his finger on the trigger in readiness and, keeping his eye on his prey, he darts out and dashes headlong toward the terrace.

As soon as he's in range, he pulls the trigger and drenches his little brother, books and all. Without taking even a moment to gloat, he turns and hightails it across the lawn all the way to an ancient oak tree at the far corner of the property where he takes cover behind its massive, gnarled trunk.

Jae Sung leaps down from his silken perch, falling on his knees and skinning them on the stone surface.

"Maaaa!!!!" he wails. He picks up his sodden workbook by its corner and regards it ruefully. Teacher will be so angry. "Maaaa!!!" he screams. In a moment, his mother rushes out through the French doors. "What on earth!" she says. She squats next to Jae Sung and examines his knees.

"Ahjumma!" she cries. "Ahjumma!"

A middle-aged housekeeper appears at the door.

"Don't just stand there," Mother says. "Bring some towels." The housekeeper scurries back into the house.

"What happened, Jae Sung?" his mother asks, wiping his wet cheeks with her hands.

"Jae Chul!" the boy chokes out through his sobs. "Of course," Mother sighs.

The housekeeper returns with towels and begins mopping up water from the table and carefully blotting the books and papers, while Mother dries off Jae Sung's arms, legs and hair.

"Teacher will be angry," Jae Sung whimpers.

"Never mind. Mother will call your teacher and explain. Stop your crying now."

"Yes, Mother," Jae Sung answers, trying hard to get his sobs under control.

"Ahjumma, take him in the house and see to his knees and get him a change of clothes. I'll finish up here."

"Yes, Madame," Ahjumma replies, taking Jae Sung by the hand and leading him inside.

Mother finishes cleaning up as best she can. She walks to the edge of the terrace and gazes out over the lawn. "Just wait till that boy comes home. Just wait."

Peering from behind the oak tree, Jae Chul smiles slyly as he admires his handiwork. That little wuss Jae Sung looks so stupid in his dripping wet shorts, bawling like a baby over his precious books. Mother is angry but she will get over it. It had all been worth it.

He ducks his head back behind the tree. Only then does he notice the small, sneakered foot tapping the ground, impatiently, reprovingly. Jae Chul starts. How did she sneak up so silently? How is she always there? He reaches up and grabs her arm, pulling her down to the ground beside him. "Get down, dummy! You're going to give me away." She stands up defiantly but at least she remains behind the tree, out of sight of the house. Jae Chul's eyes travel from the pure white sneakers, up the spindly legs and tiny body to the disapproving eyes of his nemesis, his life-long friend, his unwelcome conscience—Park Hana.

An Excerpt from Soul Rain

By Nick Torres (Eden R. Souther)

Prologue

It was long ago, before the shifting of the continents, before the humans battled for territories. It was eons before, prior to when the animals spoke of equality with man, far beyond when history and time were created. When the first dawn woke upon the Earth, the two great spirits were formed in the womb of Mother Nature. She crafted them with love and called them her sons. Then, when they were completed, she gifted them to the world.

Eirdas was the eldest son's name, and his name meant Life. Tall and noble, cascading white fur covered his body and two small wings perched on his back. His four legs tapered to points. A finely crafted ceramic mask covered his face, and two long deer-like ears poked out from behind it. The ground he walked upon erupted with flowers and vines as he passed. Energy flowed from his being and created life. His essence brought things to live upon the world his Mother had created, Aterra. The God of Life was forever loyal to his Mother. The elder was loved by all the things on Aterra and in turn, he loved all them just as much. To them, he was King and in his benevolent sight, all things prospered.

The younger son was named Paer, and his name meant Death. He had a crippled and mangled wolf-like body that held a human face with glaring red eyes, yet his heart was soft like that of a child. Where the young Spirit walked, he brought wither and decay. Because of this, the creatures to whom Eirdas had given life now feared that Paer would steal it away. This saddened Paer, for in this great world he was alone in death. Why had his brother been born glorious and noble, while he stank of rotting flesh? What had he done to deserve the hatred of the living? Confused, Paer went to the Great Mother and he pleaded for answers.

The Mother told her young son that it was because of the need for balance. Where there was light, there must also be always dark, and in their case, where there was Life, there was always Death. "Your brother is a beautiful lie, while you are a painful truth," she told him. "You are just as important as your brother." That explanation burrowed into her son like a poisoned thorn.

He was the truth and his brother was a lie.

It was on that day that an awakening occurred in the God of Death.

Life was grotesque and Death was beauty. Even if the creatures of his brother's world didn't understand, he would make them see as he did. With his Mother's words in his heart, he set out to spread the truth. So, on the first day of winter, when the darkness was longer than the light of day, Paer approached his brother. In his stride, the flowers withered and the trees lost their leaves and assumed skeletal shapes. With his breath, the air turned cool and frigid.

Death commanded that the throne be his and he be the king of Aterra. The older brother shook his head and told Paer that it was not theirs to rule. Paer began to laugh, his hysterics sounded like dying breaths. How could Eirdas say he was not the King? Surely it was another lie told by the beautiful Life.

"Brother, I promise you," Paer breathed, his voice raspy and thick with the gurgling sound of black blood. "This world will soon belong to Death." And with that, he disappeared into the growing shadows.

The older brother shook away the discomfort caused by Paer's words. Surely, he did not mean what he said. The God of Life could not understand why his brother would want to ruin the beauty they had brought to their Mother's world. Together they created balance. Why would Paer want to take that all away?

Years passed, and Eirdas continued to embellish his Mother's world. He built gardens and sights that no word could describe. The animals he formed lived as one with the land. They took only what they needed, no more and no less. Eirdas looked upon the world and he was happy. It was beautiful and grand. It was perfection in his eyes.

During this time, Paer waited, watched, and grew stronger. The God of Death counted the days for his opportunity to steal the crown of his Mother's world.

When winter returned, Paer was far more powerful than his brother, and when the day was right, when the moon reached its highest point in the sky, he confronted Eirdas. The younger Spirit's heart was heavy with a river of hatred.

"Brother," spoke Paer. "While you wasted your time and energy, I planned for this moment. I am not your equal, I am better and stronger. I can destroy what you have created. This world is mine, Eirdas."

The God of Life looked upon his brother. Hatred glowed in Paer's blood-red eyes.

Eirdas was taken aback. How had he not seen this disdain before?

"I will not allow a creature of such malice corrupt our Mother's world, Paer," said the loyal son. "I will not let you threaten the great balance."

A dark grin spread across Paer's face and he purred to his brother, "You have not the choice. For every life, there is a death, and my brother, your time is over. This kingdom is mine."

Eirdas could feel how his brother's strength had grown. Deep down, he knew he could not win, yet he could not give the world to his brother's keeping.

So, they fought.

Every attack and counter rippled the sky with thunder and cracks of lightning. Both knew the stakes at hand. The Spirit of Life knew his death was imminent and his dawn would never come. This world he had created would fall into his brother's tainted hands. Paer would kill them all for power. Eirdas could not allow that, but he knew not how to stop it.

Eirdas fell to the ground, bloody and in pain. His heart laid beating on the dusty ground.

Paer moved to his brother and tore the mask from his head. Their faces were identical. Eirdas looked up and a tear leaked from his storm- blue eye. He couldn't die here, not at his brother's hungry and ambitious hands. So, the loving benevolent Spirit uttered a soft chant below his breath, even as his own life ebbed.

Paer, who had thought himself victorious, watched as his brother's body began to glow. Then, as if Eirdas was made of glass, his body shattered into millions of shards and fragments. They stuck into the ground, before melting and shaping together, forming six beings. Each was the embodiment of a specific element of the great Mother of All. Each took a name and a shape of an animal that Eirdas had created.

Earth: the strength to shift the world and the power over the rocks and trees belonged to Sero, a young and powerful dragon.

Air: the swiftness of the softest wind and the ferociousness of the greatest tornado, was granted to the great hawk spirit, Wintaka.

Water: the serene grace of the simplest stream, but with the strength of all the oceans, was gifted to a noble Stag spirit whose name was Onimo.

Fire: the destructive force of flames that could burn eternally, was born upon a soul of a Human being, Pyran.

The last two elements were that of balance: Light and Dark. Both held the same sleek shape of a wolf. As said before, where there is light there is dark, and where there was dark, there was light. Each of these beings held this quality. The embodiment of Dark was named Alaria, and Light was known as Solaris.

In the moment when each of the great Spirits was born, they looked upon the rotting Paer; their gleaming eyes held the magnificence of stars. In unison, they spoke, "Your black heart has tainted and destroyed you. This world will never be yours. You are master of none. For your deceit and treason, you are banished from this plane of his world; you are to be banished to a place where your hate cannot harm anyone any longer."

Then, with the combined powers of their world, the six Spirits imprisoned Paer in the core of the Earth. Bound by chains of each element, seals were drawn on each link to bind the great and terrible being so that he would never harm their world again.

When the fighting ceased, each of the six Spirits continued to create the world as their Father would have. It wasn't as grand; they weren't perfect. Flaws speckled the earth. Mountains would often explode with fire, and the wind and water would team together to create terrible storms.

Despite its imperfections, their world was still full of life and when they could do no more, the Spirits disappeared into the sky. On this day, lights danced through the night with every color the eye could see. Thus, Aterra was left to fend for itself, to thrive or to perish. Even when gone, these six Spirits watched to make sure that the God of Death never returned.

An Excerpt from October Shadows

By Brennan Stidham (Eden R Souther)

Chapter 2

"It'll be good for you sweetie, I promise." Mom placed a steaming mug of coffee beside my pancakes. The foam had been artfully poured to make a series of hearts inside of hearts. The sentiment was as sweet as the drink itself.

After an appreciative sip, I cut off a piece of pancake and swirled it around in the syrup. "I don't see why I have to go to a support group." I set down the fork before I could take the bite. "I've never had an issue with being adopted. Plenty of people are."

"Think of it as a good way to meet people." Mom leaned on the counter and took a long gulp of her own beverage. "After all, they all lost their parents on the same day you lost yours."

When I was younger, the story had been fascinating to me. The details were always fuzzy. Neither one of my adoptive parents seemed to know the whole story. But at some point, I'd decided that instead of focusing on something that I could never possibly learn the truth about, I would enjoy every moment I had. Whoever my biological parents had been, I was sure that they would have wanted me to experience as much as I could in my life.

I fixed my mom with a serious look. "You and dad are my parents." I meant that more than anything. They were the ones who had taught me about the world and let me experience the vibrance that it could offer.

Why they had decided to come back to the stifling small town they had escaped from, I couldn't be sure.

"I know sweetie," she smiled, "but I think it's worth going at least once." "I'm only going to stick out," I sighed and cut off another piece of pancake. "I don't fit into the small-town aesthetic. There are more rusted pickup trucks than people. I don't agree with their views on guns, or where they belong, or any of their politics in general. On top of all of that,

I'm not going to church to have closed minded bigots yell at me about sin and how it's wrong to love."

Mom slid into the seat next to me. She placed a warm hand on my back. "You don't know that. Both your father and I grew up here, and you know we don't think like that." She gave me a loving look. "They could surprise you, but you have to give them the chance."

"You're right." As always, she was, of course. "I'll give them a chance." "Thank you." She beamed at me. My heart filled with warmth. That smile had always chased away all the bad things since I'd been little. It was a reminder that no matter how terrible things got, I always had her to protect me. "Why don't you get dressed? Dr. Melchior should be here soon. He offered to give you a ride, so that he could introduce you to the

group in a way that they would be more responsive to."

I placed my plate in the sink, then pressed a kiss into her cheek. "Thank you for the pancakes." I made my way upstairs through the still unfamiliar halls to my room. Most of my possessions remained stashed in the boxes labeled in mom's cursive script. I wandered over to one of the boxes marked 'Cata's Clothes.' From the options I had in front of me, there was little I could find in the way of cool weather clothing.

Layers would have to suffice for now.

With a sigh, I poked my head out of my doorway. "Mom, we need to go shopping for clothes soon. Isn't it supposed to get down into the 60s this week?"

"We can go tomorrow," Mom called back over the rush of the sink. "Thank you." I shut my door. She didn't have to tell me twice.

As if it wasn't a struggle to wake up three hours earlier than my body was used to, it was almost 20 degrees colder in Ashburn than back home. My only real option was to make do. I located the longest cardigan I owned from the depths of the first box. The sweater went down to my calves and would provide some kind of warmth. The only top I could find that would match was a tank top. The bottom of the top was then tucked into a pair of high-waisted floral print shorts. The delicate pattern stuck out on the deep purple fabric. For my legs, I acquired thigh-high socks, and finally a pair of black suede boots that came to my ankles.

The bag I tucked my phone into matched the shade of my shorts perfectly. I added on some gold jewelry inlaid with amethyst, then checked my reflection in the mirror. A natural look for my hair would be fine. To be safe, I pulled on a black beanie. At least that could keep some of the heat from escaping.

Satisfied, I made my way back to the kitchen.

Standing there, talking to my mother, was a stunning blonde-haired man. For a brief moment, I was sure that some movie star had somehow snuck along on our moving trip. I shook that thought from my head and realized that it must have been the doctor. Now, that was not what I'd thought of when she'd mentioned him. He had to be thirty, at the oldest, and handsome in so many different ways.

For a start, he dressed far better than any single person I'd had the fortune of seeing. His clothing was well pressed and tailored to fit his form in ways one didn't expect in a tiny town like this.

"Oh, Cat!" Mom gestured at the man who put the statue of David to shame. "This is Dr. Melchior."

The doctor held up his hand; whether it was in greeting or to stop her I didn't know. "Please. Call me Altan." He flashed a million-dollar smile. "There's no need for formality. We're going to be spending quite a bit of time together, so I'd rather start on a more personable level. I'd rather you see me as a friend than as a doctor."

"It's nice to meet you, then, Altan." I grabbed my mug and took a swig of my coffee. "I'm Ca—"

"Cataryna," he finished for me. "I know. I've heard a lot about you from your mother. I helped ensure that you had a loving home with your parents. But I also know that you'll fit in well with our group."

With his youthful appearance, I couldn't see how that was possible. Either Ashburn had better plastic surgeons than the many available in Beverly Hills, or time had treated him well. It had almost left him untouched. Another sip finished off my coffee and helped distract me from a somewhat stunned state.

"Can I get you a drink, Altan?" my mother asked, "We have coffee, juice, milk…" As she took a half step towards the refrigerator, he shook his head.

"Thank you very much for the offer, but I think Cat and I ought to be heading out." Altan put his hands into the pockets of his designer dress pants. It seemed a more likely chance that he would be leaving for a fashion show, rather than going to host a group meeting. He looked like he was about to jump onto a runway in Milan or Paris.

Just how did he fit in this Podunk little town?

Mom walked around the counter and wrapped her arms around me. "Have fun, alright?" She kissed the top of my head and squeezed me close. With one hand she took my empty mug, and with the other, she held me. Her eyes implored me to give these kids a chance.

"Of course." I tightened my grip and nodded. "I'll see you afterwards." Altan showed me out to his car, which was just as meticulously maintained as his appearance. It was sleek, shiny, and chrome.

My jaw dropped. "You have a Rolls-Royce Ghost?" My voice

came out in a high-pitched squeak.

"You're a car enthusiast?" He raised one manicured eyebrow. "Chyeah," I grazed my fingertips across the glossy paint job. This car

cost over three hundred thousand. I'd never thought I'd see a car this expensive up close. The interior still had that new car smell. I felt out of place in second hand vintage clothing on the heated tan leather seats.

A charming smile graced his lips as he buckled himself in. "Remind me to show you my full collection one day."

All I could do was nod. My awe had left me mute.

The doctor zoomed off the second I was buckled in. "I hope you don't mind if I play some music." Altan pressed a button on the steering wheel and the car was filled with the sounds of soulful classical music. Vivaldi's Four Seasons. It was encouraging to have a familiar song coming from the speakers.

He didn't try to initiate conversation; he just focused on the road.

Left alone with my thoughts, I couldn't help but dwell on my destination. Eight new strangers, who all shared the same mysterious history. This didn't honestly seem like the best way to make friends. In fact, I could easily come up with a dozen superior alternatives if I tried. But it was sort of my only option in terms of normal human interaction. We didn't have internet at the house, and from the moment we'd reached town, I'd had no cell signal. No communication with the outside world was going to be torture.

Maybe Mom was right. I could click with someone there, and actually make my first friend.

My positive attitude faded somewhat when I arrived.

I wasn't entirely surprised when the group treated me like I had The Plague. It was the mentality of the small group; the unknown is not to be trusted. I was just about as unknown as was possible for them.

Somehow, they hadn't been real until I saw their faces. Of course, I knew I wasn't the only one who'd lost my family, but hypothetical "other kids" had faded into the background of the tale for me after I realized I'd probably never meet them. While I wasn't sure what I'd expected, it wasn't such a wide range of ages, sizes, and backgrounds. I felt ignorant for assuming that there was no cultural diversity in Ashburn.

My insides squirmed as they stared at me in distressing silence. Even when I'd taken a seat, they still seemed uncomfortable.

One notable exception was the red-haired girl. She didn't even so much as glance my way. She was lost in her own little world in the clouds. Well, she had a massive orange one around her head. A dreamy expression covered her freckled face.

The pink haired guy—Skylar—seemed nice enough. Very nice, and cute. At least someone was brave enough to try to break the mold. Though if I was honest, there wasn't an unattractive face in the mix.

Altan clapped his hands together to get our attention. "Alright." He had a huge smile on his face. "Let's get started, everyone. I thought we could begin with introductions so that we can make Cataryna feel right at home. Who would like to go first? We can do it on a volunteer basis, so that no one feels uncomfortable."

I glanced around at the group. It seemed like it would be up to me to break the ice. "I can go first," I offered, "seeing how everyone else already knows each other." That, and the suspicious looks hadn't been wiped off of their faces yet.

"That's a great idea." Altan gestured for me to start. "How about your name, your age, and a little bit about yourself?"

I pushed myself up to my feet and waved. "So, I'm Cataryna, or Cat, or Cata, or Ryna, whatever you prefer; I'll respond to all of them." I rocked back onto the heels of my boots and felt them sink into the soft earth beneath me. It wasn't hard to keep a smile on my face. "I'm seventeen, and I'm from California. Okay, well I was born here, but we moved out there when I was little. I love the beach, old movies, thrifting, and well a bunch of other stuff that I don't have time to list off."

Skylar perked up. "California? That's awesome. I've always wanted to see the ocean."

"It's worth the trip; the ocean is the best," I affirmed. Skylar was definitely turning out to be the most social of the lot. I wasn't sure if that was because he was nice, a flirt, or a bit of both. I was starting to lean towards "both." I sank back down into the chair and tugged at the tops of my socks to keep them from slipping down past my knees.

"Why don't you go next Skylar?" Altan urged.

Skylar maneuvered the red-head out of his lap, then hopped out of his seat and gave a showy bow. "My name is Skylar, I'm eighteen, almost nineteen. I live with my mom and I'm currently a bum, cuz I'm not going to school and there's nowhere to work'n'stuff." He shrugged. "I'm still trying to figure life out." The pink haired boy winked at me, then flopped back down.

Absolutely a bit of both.

"Thank you, Skylar." Altan flashed a perfect grin.

The next person to speak up was the young woman with the toddler in her arms who had so graciously given me her spot. "My name is Thema." She rocked her child. "And this is little Autumn. I'm twenty-two, and I'm married to this cutie." She winked at the man that had to be her husband. Her southern twang was just the sort of thing I'd expected to hear from everyone. "I'm also the town's beautician, so if you ever need a styling, I'm your woman." She bobbed her head to signal that she had finished.

"Since she called me out…" Thema's husband rose to his feet and put an arm around her. "I'm Galen Antonio, but I prefer Anthony or Tony. I'm also twenty-two, and I'm the papa of that little precious princess. I have a degree in agriculture, and I help the local farmers with their fields." His liquid chocolate eyes sparkled in the fire light.

He gave his wife a kiss on the cheek before he offered Thema his seat. The young woman who I could only begin to explain as a goth vampire girl let out a sigh and ran a hand through her short dark hair. "I'm Willow, twenty and I'm in college studying art." Her stunning monolid

eyes immediately returned to the pad of paper in her lap.

"Thank you Willow. That was very informative." Altan gave a low chuckle.

An involuntary shiver went up my spine. It wasn't from the cold, or so I thought. I glanced around the circle and found myself staring into the vivid green eyes of the red-haired girl. She had a blank expression on her face, but her stare was intense. I could feel it drilling into me even from across the circle.

In the space of a blink, she was back to watching the clouds.

I turned my attention to the fire to shake away the awkward moment. The bonfire had calmed down. The flames only flickered as high as our knees. It provided enough warmth for all of us. Or at least I assumed it did. It felt nice to me.

From beside Willow, the other quiet girl rose to her feet. She had rich mahogany hair and bright hazel eyes. She had on jeans and a knit sweater that all worked well with her calf-high boots. She had a friendly smile on her face. "My name is River. I'm seventeen, and a senior in high school. I'm president of the Art Club and co-captain of Show Choir. I can show you around the school on Monday if you'd like."

After getting the southern charm from Skylar, it was nice to get some southern hospitality from both Thema and River. "That would be amazing. Thank you."

The boy with the soccer ball tossed it into the air, then caught it again. "My name is Korin, and I just turned nineteen. I'm going to school on a soccer scholarship." He looked like a lot of soccer players I'd known. Korin seemed like the kind of person who only spent time inside because he was obligated to.

It was quiet as the last two battled on who would have to speak up next. The silent war raged, but only one of the parties was even aware that it was going on. So, it was left to the girl with the scarf to go. It was hard to hear her through the protective wrap, "I'm Lu. I'm fifteen, and I like animals, unicorns, and candy. I like to sew and make s'mores. And touching Skylar's hair, because it's pink, and I like pink soft things."

"It looks like all we have left is Nyssa." Altan turned his attention to the red headed girl.

"Oh. Hmm?" Nyssa's gaze left the clouds. "My turn?" Her eyelids fluttered for a few seconds before she rose to her feet. "I'm Nyrissa, Nyssa is what everyone calls me. I'm eighteen and I am home-schooled. I haven't decided what to do with the rest of my life yet, however long that may be." Then she sunk back into her chair as though she'd just said something completely normal.

Her comment left me stunned. I had expected something like that from Willow, but not Nyssa. Her pessimism seemed like it could have been part of a deeper problem, yet no one else seemed bothered by it.

Altan appeared to be content with everyone's introductions so he gave that same smile again. "Thank you everyone, that was lovely. So, how have things been in the last week? Does anyone have any issues they'd like to discuss with the group?"

When no one spoke up, Altan turned his attention to me. "What about you Cat? How has your experience with moving been?"

"Moving is always stressful." I shrugged. "I miss home, but I guess this will just get to be a new adventure. I can make new friends, and at the end of the year, I'll go to college and get to start another new journey. That's what life is about, after all, right?"

Warmth rolled up the back of my neck as the others just stared at me. It was hard to maintain the calm when their judgement rolled off in waves. It never used to bother me.

Yet with ten pairs of eyes focused on me, I felt an anxiety I hadn't before. Heat rolled through my chest and filled my lungs. It surged up my throat and choked my words off. I couldn't begin to understand why it was coming, but it wouldn't stop. My nails dug into my chair. My stomach constricted into knots. My whole body was starting to shake. Each beat of my heart thundered in my ears.

Just as I thought I was going to burst, there was a crack. Flames from the bonfire shot into the air high above our heads. Someone screamed.

The next thing I knew Thema was rubbing Nyssa's back. "It's ok, sweetie, a log fell over." Her tone was motherly, and warm. "There's nothing to be scared about."

Nyssa was ghostly pale; she was shaking. But the sound of Thema's voice brought her down. She slowly returned to the spacy look I'd come to assume was just her default and gave Thema a hug. "Thanks mama," I heard her mutter.

"I think it's a lovely sentiment, Cat," Altan added in an attempt to get everything back on track.

"Thanks." I ran a hand through my hair. The feeling was gone. I was just thankful the attention had been taken off of me.

"Anyone else?" the doctor asked.

A cold snort grabbed everyone's attention. "Isn't Sky going to complain for the rest of the hour?" Korin had turned his focus to the pink-haired Skylar with a smirk on his face. "You know, like every other time?"

Skylar crossed his arm and pouted. "You're so mean to me!" He paused, "But okay. So, Linda broke into my computer, so she could spy on my history and downloads. When she was done, I guess she didn't like what she found 'cause she dumped her glass of wine on it. So now it's busted, and I'm hosed."

"I'm sure there's a way to restore it," Altan soothed. "I could give you a ride to the tech store in Rutledge as soon as we can to get it fixed up."

"You sure you don't mind?" Skylar perked up. "That's like an hour away, and I know you're busy."

Altan shook his head. "I don't mind. I know how important the laptop is to you." He leaned back in his seat. "I have to run some errands anyway, so it's no trouble." It was refreshing to see the doctor being so tender towards the other kids. He was definitely growing on me.

They kept talking, and I took some vague notes on their basic interactions and possible relationships that they shared together. A few of them complained about their parents, but I couldn't begin to understand. My parents were perfect. Well, at least they seemed normal. They treated me like their own. I hadn't even known that I was adopted until I was ten. All the while, I couldn't help but continue to return back to the fire. I hadn't seen the log fall, and I'd never seen a flame leap that high in the air before. It had easily reached clear over Tony's head. I'd had my fair share of bonfires on the beach and even then, it never shot that high. Was it the kind of wood, or the cold air or something? Yeah, that had to be it.

I had other things to focus on, like the fact that I had to start over in a new school. Yet, I couldn't say I understood the small-town mentality any better. If my parents asked about school I couldn't use the "I don't know anyone" excuse. Maybe River and I would become friends. She was the only other one who'd been friendly.

Maybe living here would be alright.

Plays

The Roast of Eliot Ness
By Tim Crawford

THE ROAST OF ELIOT NESS,
OR A COMEDY YOU CAN'T REFUSE

Enter LOIS LANE with handheld microphone.

LOIS LANE

Hello, Metropolis! How you doing tonight?

> (Lois may need to ad lib something to engage the audience, perhaps: "You can do better than that. I said 'How you doing tonight?' That's better.")

I'm Lois Lane, and I'll be your Roastmaster of Ceremonies for the evening. Hopefully, you will all know me from my byline as an award- winning reporter for the Daily Planet. But if you only know me as Superman's girlfriend, well, that's okay too, you sexist pig!

> (If any man in the audience reacts to her Superman reference, she could point in their direction.)

Just kidding. So, why have I gathered you all here tonight? First, it's Valentine's Day. Second, everybody loves a good roast, right? But who to roast? Then, I saw an article about the battle over plans to name their new DC headquarters the Eliot Ness ATF Building. Historian Daniel Okrent found the idea ridiculous, saying "Naming a building after Ness for his role in getting Capone? You might as well name it after Batman."

> (Lois give a big smile with some eyebrow action.)

That was enough for me. So, welcome to the centerpiece of this charity event. A comedy you can't refuse, the roast of Eliot Ness! So, let's

(MORE)
LOIS LANE (CONT'D)

pretend that Superman plucked a bunch of iconic legends from the past and brought them here for your entertainment. Let's welcome our Roasters!

> (Lane, or someone else, holds up an applause sign and she keeps talking over the applause.)

The legendary Ms. Bonnie Parker!

> (Enter BONNIE PARKER. Parker blows a kiss and sits on sofa stage left. Enter PRETTY BOY FLOYD.)

Pretty Boy Floyd!

> (Floyd also blows a kiss and sits on the sofa stage left. Enter AL CAPONE with a baseball bat.)

Big Al Capone!

> (Capone brandishes the baseball bat menacingly, before smiling and waiving to the crowd. He sits on the sofa.)

Are you ready for our guest of honor?

> (If necessary, Lane repeats "I said, are you ready for our guest of honor?")

Lets hear it for the man who made being an untouchable sound like a good thing, everybody's favorite pro-inhibition agent, Eliot Ness!

> Lane leads the audience in applause as ELIOT NESS enters, soaks in the applause, and fist bumps with Lane.

ELIOT NESS

Thank you, thank you. A gift for you, a first edition of my memoir, The Untouchables.

> Ness looks at the Roasters with contempt, and takes a seat on the Iron Throne made of tommy guns and rifles, upstage center.

LOIS LANE

Agent Ness, it's an honor to have you here with us tonight. You are an iconic lawman, the inspiration for books, TV shows, movies,

---

and yes, comic books, too. But still no action figures or PlayStation games. So, when it comes to those, my boyfriend, Clar--, um, Superman is "untouchable." Mr. Ness you grew up living at 10811 South Prairie Avenue in Chicago. Your father had lots of dough, or more accurately,

I should say he owned a bakery. It's a little known fact that Al Capone, who ran a criminal enterprise called, the Chicago Outfit, lived just a few block away on the same street for a couple of years, according to your Wikipedia page, until your parents moved to a new house in 1928. That's shocking, because it means, wow, while you were point man on bringing down Public Enemy #1, you were living with your Mommy.

Okay, let's bring up our first Roaster. You know her, you love her. She's a poet, romantic legend, and feminist anti-hero, who was also associated with a male chauvinist named Clyde Barrow. Please give her a warm welcome, Ms. Bonnie Parker!

Parker shakes hands with Lane and crosses to a lectern, stage right of the Iron Throne. Lane goes to sit with the other Roasters.

BONNIE PARKER

Lois Lane, everybody! Lois Lane.

(Leads the audience in applause.)

Lois, I've always, uh, wondered how you and Superman..., you know...

(Lois stops her with a look and a gesture.)

Hey, you bunch of stool pigeons and rats out there! Don't worry, though, I'm going convert you to my henchmen, before I go. I'm up here with the biggest name in crime, Mr. Al Capone. But before I found out this guy was Al Capone, I was, like, who's the fat guy. What'd he do, rob a pasta factory? Most people don't know this, but he's the only prisoner to "escape" Alcatraz. Well, he didn't dig a tunnel or anything. They let him out because he had regressed to the mentality of a 12-year- old child due to paralytic dementia or P.D., which he got from V.D., which kids nowadays call STDs. I'm not sure who that other guy over there is, but dang, you sure are pretty. Too bad you're also not smarter than a six-grader. When I was telling you how the Feds pinned every crime on the Barrow

gang, (MORE)
    BONNIE PARKER (CONT'D)
except the Lindbergh kidnapping. You said "is that because he woke
up?" Mr. Ness, we never met, but we have something in common.
We both used our writings, even if you used a ghostwriter, to create
our legend. I wrote poetry. Unfortunately, The Untouchables didn't
get published while you were living. And you never got to watch
Kevin Costner, as you, throw Frank Nitti off a rooftop. Which made
you out to be kind of a... murderer. Three, two, one!

            As Parker reaches "one," Capone and Floyd stand.

                    CAPONE/FLOYD/PARKER
Welcome to the club!

                        BONNIE PARKER
                        (To the audience.)
Well, I hope I've converted some of you stool pigeons. Good night,
henchmen!

                            Lane crosses toward Parker. They hug.
                            Parker returns to her seat. Lane goes to the
                            lectern.

                        LOIS LANE

Bonnie Parker, everybody! Our next Roaster has been called the
Robin Hood of the Sagebrush. He's Pretty Boy Floyd.

                            Floyd crosses to the lectern. Lane offers a
                            stiffly extended arm for a perfunctory hand
                            shake.

                    PRETTY BOY FLOYD

I never cared for that moniker. I hear there's more'n 200 folks on
Twitter calling theirselves Pretty Boy Floyd. Who'd have thunk it?
There's even more on Grindr.

                            (Depending on the response, Floyd might
                            start to explain the joke: "You see, that's
                            because Grindr is a gay dating app, so there's

more ")

We got the notorious Al Capone here tonight, everybody. Mr. Capone, for a fella who ran an operation called the Chicago Outfit, I reckoned you'd be a better dresser. Bonnie, I'm gonna be a gentleman and simply say, I hope somehow you'll go far, and I really hope you stay there. Mr. Ness, I had hoped to never meet you, so I figured to give you a nasty look, but I see you already got one. As you know, Mr. Ness, Pretty Boy is not the name on my tax form. That's right, Mr. Capone, I filed my taxes. What a concept, eh?

(He holds up one sheet of paper.)

Here's my 1933 tax papers. Made no money, owes no taxes. It's signed, Charles Arthur Floyd. That's my real name. The great Woodie Guthrie didn't know that when he wrote The Ballad of Pretty Boy Floyd, a song about my fracas with a sheriff in Shawnee and a starvin' farmer who's mortgage was paid by an outlaw.

(Points to himself.)

My favorite part of the song is the end: "...as through you life you roam,/ You won't never see an outlaw/ Drive a family from their home." The bankers was the bad guys, jest like today. I'm looking at you Chase United Mileage Plus Explorer Card.

BONNIE PARKER
(Laughing and out of character.)
That's awfully specific, [actor portraying Floyd's real first name].

PRETTY BOY FLOYD

Oops!

(Realizing he's out of character. Regains his folksy tone.)

Folks would sometimes call me "Choc," after my fondness for home-brewed Choctaw beer. I drank a lotta beer. I like beer. I used to drink beer with my buds, Tobin and Squi. We all ignored Prohibition and continued "boofing" and playing the Devil's Triangle.

What's that?

PRETTY BOY FLOYD

Heh heh! I'll show ya later, Bonnie. Mr. Ness, tonight is your night, and I want you to know, I have had a perfect evening, but tonight wasn't it. Goodnight, everybody!

> Floyd crosses left back to his seat. Lane talks while crossing back to the lectern.

LOIS LANE

Pretty Boy Floyd, everybody.

> (She applauds. Floyd glares at her for using the nickname. Lois shivers.)

Ooh! I feel a sudden chill in the air.

> We hear the ghostly howl of the ghost of OSCAR FRALEY, before he enters.

OSCAR FRALEY

Woooooooo! Woooooooo!

LOIS LANE

Who are you?

OSCAR FRALEY

I'm the ghost of Oscar Fraley!

ELIOT NESS

Oh my god, that's the ghost of my ghostwriter.

LOIS LANE

Why this visitation tonight, Mr. Fraley?

OSCAR FRALEY

I'm haunting your asses, because I should have been a roaster for my old pal, Eliot.

Capone is ill at ease in the presence of this apparition. He starts looking for his baseball bat.

OSCAR FRALEY

Wait — no. I meant to say... I mean...

LOIS LANE

You have material?

OSCAR FRALEY

Of course. In life, I was a sports writer with daily deadlines. Woops, deadlines. I probably shouldn't use that word. I also wrote two sequels to The Untouchables. So, yeah, I always have material.

(Lois backs away from the lectern to allow Fraley to step up. Fraley, looks out at the audience.)

Buckle up, bitches, I'm about to bring the funny.

(Addressing the panel of Roasters on the sofa.)

Look at you! Is this a roast or the cast of a 1930's stag film?

Floyd likes this joke and laughs. Capone is growing more agitated.

OSCAR FRALEY

Did you all know that Eliot Ness was once in charge of the police in Cleveland?

AL CAPONE

I don't like ghosts!

Capone is up with the baseball bat and approaching Fraley. Capone starts speaking in Italian under his breath.

Translation: "I don't like ghosts. Out, I say. Out! Capone pokes Fraley with the baseball bat. Fraley recoils in pain.

OSCAR FRALEY

What!? Ouch!

Capone pokes him with the baseball bat again. It's subtle, but Capone's words are what banish the ghost, not the bat.

AL CAPONE

Out, I say!

OSCAR FRALEY

Ow! That hurts.

> Fraley covers his ears, and exits the stage
> quickly.

LOIS LANE
(Tentatively.)
The ghost of Oscar Fraley, everybody.
> (Lane takes the baseball bat from Capone,
> who uses the moment to shake off his
> encounter with the ghost.)
Ladies and Gentlemen, now we have our final Roaster the evening.
> (Lois uses the Italian pronunciation of
> "Capone" [kah-PONE-eh] in her
> introduction.)
Here he is, the O.G. Scarface, Alphonso "Big Al" Capone!

AL CAPONE
Thank you, Miss Lane. Have your boyfriend stop by the restaurant.
I've got some nice pasta fazool on the menu laced with... Kryptonite.
Capeesh?
> (He laughs.)
I'm kidding, I kid Superman. I kid all our extraterrestrial overlords.
But seriously, I like the big blue Boy Scout. You see, I'm not a
Boy Scout or a choir boy. I'm a successful Italian business man in
a tough business. Sometimes I think, you know, I really wanted to
be in the milk business. More people bought milk than beer and
the markup, much higher. But I didn't change rackets, because I
was sure if I died in the milk business, the papers would say I had
reached my "expiration date." When the 18th Amendment passed,
nobody thought the words in there "intoxicating liquors" included
the prohibition of beer and wine. Surprise, America! The Volstead
Act officially made the USA
a dry country in January 1920, and at the same time turned on the
spigot for illegal booze and organized crime. As a result, we got the
likes of Bonnie and Clyde and Pretty Boy Floyd.
(MORE)

AL CAPONE (CONT'D)

Bonnie, Ms. Parker, after meeting you I must say, I envy people who have never met you. I had the misfortune to read some of your poetry. You know, I could eat a bowl of alphabet soup and poop out a better poem. Mr. Floyd, after hearing your "jokes," I can safely say that you're not the dumbest person on the planet, but you sure better hope he don't die.

> (Depending on the reaction, Capone could start to explain the joke, "you see, that's because there's just one person on the planet who is dumber and...")

They used to say bootlegging was a gateway crime that led to prostitution, gambling, and loan-sharking. Funny thing though, these days gambling is legal everywhere. Pretty Boy, you coulda played your IQ in the Pick 2 tonight. What we called loan-sharking, you now call "credit card debt." You knew something was wrong during Prohibition, because America somehow became the biggest importer of cocktail shakers in the world. We were all scofflaws. So, why pick on me Mr. Ness? Was it jealousy? Is it because I was a celebrity? They told me I should bring some sick burns to this Roast instead of my baseball bat, but I brought both. So, now, I'm gonna sic Ken Burns on ya, Mr. Ness. They asked Ken Burns why Eliot Ness is never mentioned in his six- hour documentary on Prohibition? Burns said that's because "Eliot Ness is a PR invention." Ouch! I was world famous in my time, a darling of the press. I hear you ran for mayor in Cleveland and lost, and you came to be known as a womanizer. So, you traded truth, justice and the American way for Ruth, Justine and the occasional three-way. Turns out being known as the richest man in "Crook" County put me on the fast track to Alcatraz. The only thing they could get me on was back taxes. Whoop-de-do! I guess it was my own fault. Publicity, that's what really got me. Not you, Ness. Cubs players would come over to get my autograph at Wrigley Field. If Instagram had been around then, I would have been a hashtag IG model. Like a Kardashian without the gazongas.

> (Pause.)

I have no idea what that means. In closing, I want all of you young people out there to remember this: fame is fleeting, but embarrassing Tweeting is forever. Goodnight everybody!

Mr. Al Capone, everyone.

> (She leads the audience in applause and speaks before the applause dies.)

Ladies and gents, we are blessed, so to speak, to have with us in the audience, someone who may have a bone to pick with you, Mr. Capone. Say "halo" to Saint Valentine.

> ST. VALENTINE stands in the audience. He holds something in a box.

ST. VALENTINE

Thank you, Lois. As the saint of lovers, I must say, you've taken things to a place I hadn't even considered. I mean, your boyfriend! He's, like, a space alien from the planet Krypton, right?

> (He makes a hand gesture to suggest that his brain just exploded.)

PUH-SHOOM!

LOIS LANE

Let's not go there. What's in the box?

PRETTY BOY FLOYD
> (He whines like Brad Pitt in Se7en.)

What's in the box?

ST. VALENTINE

Interesting story! There were actually two St. Valentines. We were both executed on the same day in the year 270. We were close. Unfortunately, he was beheaded.

> (Points to the box.)

But we remain close.

BONNIE PARKER

Ewww!

ST. VALENTINE

When you were just Little Al, we thought getting kicked out of Catholic school for hitting a teacher in the face would be the worse thing you'd do.

(MORE)

ST. VALENTINE (CONT'D)

Boy, were we wrong! You did some messed up stuff. Then you really crossed the line. You had seven members of the Bugs Moran gang machine gunned to death on my day, St. Valentines Day. What were you thinking?! You put taint on my day and, if not for you, we wouldn't have those reprehensible My Bloody Valentine slasher films. I have to carry my head in shame because of you. Which is ironic because...

(His voice trails off as he holds up the box, which probably contains a severed head.)

I have to, you know, literally carry "my" head.

LOIS LANE

Thank you, Saint--

ST. VALENTINE

Wait, there's more.

LOIS LANE

Oh, sorry.

ST. VALENTINE

I want to say to you, Ms. Bonnie Parker, bless you, my dear. I notice that you mention me in one of your poems. This gives me the opportunity to say: Leave me the hell out of it! Please. I don't need the bad PR of being associated with gangsters and bank robbers. You know, it's hard out here for a saint. I'm trying to make the world a better place for righteous lovers. It's like being the Christian Mingle app in a Pornhub world. But make no mistake, I'm the saint of romance that you all deserve, even though, I know you think Tinder is the one you need. Peace and love.

LOIS LANE

St. Valentine, everybody. They say, not all heroes wear a cape, and maybe that saying came to be because of our guest of honor, Mr. Eliot Ness!

Lane leads the audience in applause. Ness steps off the throne, doffs his hat, bows to the crowd and goes to the lectern. Lane joins the Roasters on the sofa.

ELIOT NESS

Thank you, Lois Lane. Please say hello to your boyfriend for me. He'd be my hero, except I became my own hero, as immodest as that sounds, along with my Untouchables, when we showed law enforcement in America that the best cops money can buy can't be bought. Miss Bonnie Parker, they say your life was like a fairy tale. By that I mean, you're like Rapunzel, except instead of letting down your hair, you let down everybody in your life. Mr. Pretty Boy Floyd, you're not pretty enough to be that dumb. I hear you're so dumb you once sold your car for gas money. Scarface, I know you don't like that nickname but, spoiler alert, that's the nicest thing I'm going to say about you tonight. The New York Times once called you "a monstrous symbol of a disease which was eating into the conscience of America." Ironically, at the same time, syphilis was eating away at your brain. Big Al, many people, including you, apparently, thought you would die at the barrel of a gun. Turns out you were only shot once, and it was by a notorious gangster by the name of Al Capone. That's right! While you were golfing in 1928, a pistol went off in your pocket, wounding you in your scrotum. Yikes! And to add injury to insult, you endured more, uh, genital trauma the following year in Philadelphia, where you were locked up on a concealed weapons charge (geez, will you ever learn), when prison doctors in Philadelphia, said "hello" to your "little friend" with a scalpel when they circumcised you in a failed attempt to cure your syphilis. Ouchies!

(Floyd winces and crosses his legs.)

It's true you did try to bribe me. You offered to put $2,000 on my desk every Monday. That'd be a whopping $33,000 a week in today's dollars. I turned that down. But it gave me an idea for a different tactic to jail you, making you account for that money. People will say "you got him on tax evasion, not murder or gambling or bootlegging." Yeah, I'm sure you told all the bad guys in Alcatraz, "hey, I'm not a killer. I'm in here because TurboTax sucks." Yes, I brought you down for tax evasion, but I also indicted you on 5000 criminal violations of the Volstead Act, which would be like a million felonies and 5 health-code infractions in today's crime statistics.

(He continues, a little choked up at first.)

But seriously folks, I want to take a moment to thank all of you for "honoring" me here tonight.

(MORE)

Yes, tonight was all in good fun, and they sure were good at making fun of me. And yes, some will forever do so, but in the end, I will have my story and they will have theirs. Good versus evil will always demand a hero. For as long as crime and corruption are a dark cloud in the path of the disinfectant and renewing powers of sunlight, there will always emerge an untouchable hero. And if you should decide to build another big-ass statue here in Metropolis honoring a famous person with crime-fighting superpowers, a person who was the inspiration for a great comic-strip character by the name of Dick Tracy, then I know the perfect person to strike the pose for your sculptor.

> Ness steps in front of the lectern and strikes the heroic Superman pose with his fists on his hips as Lane leads audience in applause and joins Ness at the lectern.

LOIS LANE

Eliot Ness, everyone. Eliot Ness!

> (To the audience, with Ness at her side.)

Before I let you go, let's thank our Roasters and St. Valentine.

> (She claps for the Roasters, then reads from note cards, because she wants to get it right as she shares "the moral of the story" with the audience.)

Both experts and the populous agree that Prohibition was a mistake. Out of that mistake grew two amazing careers, the criminal career of Al Capone, which in turn led to the legend that was Eliot Ness, both unintended consequence of a shameful time in American history. Mr. Ness, you and your roasters have one thing in common. You all nurtured your public images, on both side of the law, to create legendary characters who have lasted long beyond your respective lifespans. But, with the exception of you, Mr. Ness, the others missed out on the most powerful aspect of being a legend. Like my boyfriend, Mr. Ness, you made the choice to use your celebrity and power to inspire others to do good, and that's how you and Superman have changed the world for the better. Goodnight everybody.

END

Non-Fiction

Strawberries
Nancy Hodge Long

When my mother passed away, I was teaching my Friday morning Yoga class. I knew she was fragile and may even had been sick. I was taking her to her pulmonary doctor later that morning. But as class began, I let go of all my external distractions, even my concern for her. Somewhere toward the end of class, my husband, Mike appeared in the doorway. His look was ominous. My first thought was something happened to his mother who was in the hospital, near death with pneumonia.

As I walked to the door, I turned to the class and said, "Go ahead and begin your meditation." When I turned back to Mike, his mouth gently curved into a painful smile and he hugged me. "Let's go into the office."

I waited for him to shut the office door to ask how his mom was. Very quietly, he told me it wasn't his mom, but mine that had died. She was on the way to the ER. In an ambulance with strangers, my mother drew her last breath. My heart felt as if a dagger had been thrust into it. I dropped to my knees and wailed like a baby. Mike gently held me in his arms with tenderness and compassion. He loved my mother, too, and I think maybe he knew I would be doing this for him soon as well.

When we arrived at the ER, we were led to one of rooms where she had been left. My sister was already there and recognizing each other's tears, we embraced in our shared grief. They let us stay for as long as we wanted. I was able to recite a prayer from the Tibetan Book of the Dead and say farewell to my mother. I could feel her presence still there, but her body was stiff and lifeless. Her face beheld a peace and ease I had not seen in her when she was alive.

As we began to consider all the things we needed to do, I volunteered to go back to the facility where she had been staying. The most difficult walk I've ever made was the one from the entrance to her room. As I stood looking at the now empty bed, it began to sink in ~ she's really gone.

One of the nurses (I think her name was Corrine) who had been so good with her came by and gave me a hug. She began to tell me what had happened that morning. Mom had asked if she could have breakfast in her room because she wasn't feeling very well. Corrine brought her a tray with food, including strawberries. When she returned, my mother told her they were the best strawberries she had ever eaten. Ten minutes later, she was gasping for her breath unable to talk.

They tried to reach both my sister & me, but we were not answering. So they called Mike and he said, "Yes, call the ambulance. I'll notify her daughters and meet them at the hospital." The paramedics said she had stopped breathing enroute and of course, at 88, with COPD, she had a "do not resuscitate" order in her file.

As it turned out, I was grateful I had gone back to her room so soon after her death. The nurse was able to tell me details I might not have received had I waited a day or more. Now I have a wonderful memory of my mother enjoying those last few moments of her life. I mean, really, how much more could you be in the present moment than when enjoying the best strawberries you ever had...

http://nanyoga-alongthepath.blogspot.com

The Great Mystery
Nancy Hodge Long

My mother died in July 2009, less than a month from her 88th birthday. I miss her. She was my anchor though I never thought about it much. Her last several years brought health problems that diminished the quality of life, like a thief stealing just small things, but over and over until so little remained that she was able to do. She used to say, "Why am I still here, Nan? What use is there for me to be alive?"

To be honest, at times, I wondered that, too. But I would repeat each time she asked, "It's a mystery, Mom. No one knows why. It's the great mystery!" Then we'd laugh or sigh and talk about what was happening with the family or the latest gossip at the assisted living center where she lived. She was like a teen giggling when she told me about the man who sang "There she is... Miss America" as she slowly worked her walker through the dining room to her place at the table. She never liked attention, but I think underneath the embarrassment she remembered how beautiful she really was.

Before she died, my sisters and I were able to have a discussion about those final details. She had some papers in her desk with insurance and cemetery information, along with a folded yellow newspaper clipping. It was a poem she had kept from the local newspaper many years before. She wanted it read at her funeral. The four of us sat quietly staring at each other. I picked up that tattered piece of paper and began to read.

Do not stand at my grave and weep,
I am not there, I do not sleep.
I am in a thousand winds that blow. I am the softly falling snow.
I am the gentle showers of rain. I am the fields of ripening grain.
I am in the morning hush, I am in the graceful rush
Of beautiful birds in circling flight,
I am the starshine of the night.
I am in the flowers that bloom, I am in a quiet room.
I am the birds that sing,
I am in each lovely thing.
Do not stand at my grave and cry, I am not there, I do not die.

~Mary Frye~

I knew I wanted to read this. After a lifetime of connection with this woman I called "mother", my heart overflowed with quiet gratitude. How could I have not known who she really was? After all of my studying and practicing the non-dual teachings of Yoga...

It's a mystery! When do we realize who we really are? Is it just a glimpse or does it stay? Do we have to do anything to keep it? What happens when the body dies? Why are we so afraid? Who, exactly is afraid?

Now I watch as each moment unfolds, wondering what will this body experience? And welcoming everything just as it is ~ letting go into the great mystery.

http://nanyoga-alongthepath.blogspot.com

Daily Thoughts

Sharron Magyar

Hand to Hand

I feel your heartbeat, strong and sure,
Transmitting energy from your hand to mine.
You lend me your hand true and pure,
Your strength pouring into me from the divine,
I'm so glad you could give me a helping hand,
To lift this pain off my heart.
Just knowing someone is there to give a hand
Helps me know tomorrow is a new start.
When life gets tough, I'll always remember
The warmth of your hand
That helped to heal my heart.

Snow

Snow sticks to our eyelashes like glue.
Our noses and ears are red,
Snot dripping on the ground.
We go into the front-
Door of the house,
Tripping over fallen wet boots
And mushed up gloves,
Warming our hands by the stove.
Feeling returning
Into our hands.
It was a good morning.
All is quiet outside
Except for the tracks in the snow,
Whisper of the wind
Snow-frost glistening in the trees,
The rabbit hiding in its den.
Stillness…

Mr. Control

Meet Mr. Control. He is big, looming and always follows me around. He also has magical powers to insert thoughts into my head. What I don't like about Mr. Control is that he is a bully, and always must have his way. He is a big fat downer.

Often Mr. Control throws a tantrum and whines like a child when he can't insert himself when I am creating art. Sly and sneaky, he tells me, "that's not how you should do it". He also tells me I should have a half of a day to work on my art, a pristine clean spot and all the right tools. He is so particular and bossy.

It is not enough to control my art but thinks he should be present in my relationships with my children and grandchildren. When they are receiving some of their life lessons, he tries to, "fix things for them." I can see the kid's eyes glazing over and their ears shutting down when he talks. When will he ever learn no one can have as much control as he expects?

I have learned of late Mr. Control and my mother are alike, both are perfectionists. I love Mom. I remember as a kid cleaning up the house she came along and made me do the dishes all over again because she found a spot on one spoon. Who cares about one small spot? Sometimes Mr. Control even uses her voice.

I think I married Mr. Control. My husband stands over my shoulder watching me peel potatoes, telling me how to hold the knife. My mother never liked the way I peeled potatoes either, she thought I peeled too much of the skin off. I can feel myself rearing up to take a big hunk out of the potatoes when I think of it. Take that!

I know Mr. Control wants what is best for me. He is trying to keep me from checking out from the insanity of my inability to say no to all my creative ideas and the chaos of the world. I will give him ten minutes of each day to create a "work list". If he can help me follow through without stressing me, he can stay.

I am sorry Mr. Control for talking bad about you. I love you... give me room to be that creative, laughing, joyous me!

I Write

I write. Sometimes I cry when I write, sometimes I laugh. I write my daughters story of addiction. It is a story of the depths of despair and ultimate forgiveness. What story do I write about myself? It is continuing to unfold. I pray it reflects God's wisdom.

Boredom

"Boredom is when you forget to focus on your gifts."
- Sharron Magyar

The Ghost of Times Past

One day I find myself on an ancient Indian trail
There is me of yesterday at crossroads with me tomorrow
Walking the path of my ancestors
Feeling their dreams and sorrows
Knowing my future comes from yesterday A
s I surrender my head and pray.
Forgive us our transgressions for which we pay
Let joy in our voices sing in unison
As we bow our heads to the sun
Heal our hearts and our souls
Temper our pain, let love flow
Throughout all ages, we are one.
We are whole; we follow the sun
As we stand on this sacred ground
Let lose our battle cry
As we stand with the ghosts of times past
Grandmothers let your wailing cease
Grandfathers wipe away your sins and sorrows
Hear the drum chant and pray for peace
As we stand on this sacred ground
Meeting yesterday and tomorrow
Head held high, free from pain
For the ghosts of past are alive today
Carrying hope for humanity
With our stories of healing and grace

Dreamtime

That blissful slumber,
That alter land
Somehow seems more real
Than when I am awake
I know how I feel,
Rather than that false reality.
Alas, those thoughts are allusive,
Vanishing the moment, I am awake.
I am trying to hold on to this timeless place
For I just lost something more
Valuable than my dreamscape

Foggy Day

There was a surprise this morning
when I woke up and looked
out the window at brilliant light.
Someone came out last night
and painted the land
with
frost and fog
glistening and sparkling
against the cloudy sky.

I take a moment and breathe in
this gift given to me.
I hear the tree in it's quiet hush,
elegantly wearing its new clothes.
It looks like a princess all dressed
in her white glistening gown
ready for the ball
and I am invited.

Ghosts

I have them stacked in my closet
They're all the people I cannot forgive
They've hurt me and lied and cheated again and again
I can spend all day in my room and never be alone
For all I must do is think of my ghosts
And I'm angry all over again
They whisper, laugh, and mock me
I cannot open the door, for they will only bring pain
But I fear leaving it shut in my trembling and rage
I know I can treat others just the way they treated me
Make a ghost out of them, they disappear
But then I find I'm behind the door of my pain
A ghost lost with the rest, begging for release
Illusion and delusion substance inside me,
My spirit just a ghost locked out of reality

My Best Friend

My best friend I have lost
Inconsolable I am
I am looking at me
And I ask
Who are your crying for? I
s it you or me?
My souls asks
Why would you?
I walk hand in hand with God,

But you, your adrift at sea.

Now I Realize

Every day, I live with physical pain. I used to be confrontational
with it. "What the hell are you doing in my life?" Get out!
I have grown through the pain.
I am more compassionate with myself and others. Thank you
pain for what you have taught me about life.

Nothingness

I want nothing
I am nothing
I remember nothing
I am an empty rose
So I can be filled By the universe
With grace & love
So I can live
And love myself
To be reflected
Back to others
A time in space
Living in grace
Just me free
Petals unfolding

Light of the Moon

In the light of the moon
with darkness surrounding me
I move to the light
not knowing where I am going.
I am met by my ancestors
generation to generation
as they unveil the light,
a gift of treasure for me.
Love awaits and surrounds me
without and within.
Tears flow down my eyes,
my heart receives.
I know I am, and I can
pass this light of love to
my children and grandchildren.
The light exploding from darkness
energy and form taking place
power beyond all words
A light now in existence… I am

One moment

Grief is a tough taskmaster. She stands there with her ruler in hand, ready to pounce when my attention to the moment strays. She has disciplined me. I cannot stray my thinking to the past. "What ifs." "I should have." "If only." Remaining in the past sucks the energy out of my present. I concentrate on what is present now. One moment, one minute at a time, complete circle, here writing... now.

Lilacs

Going to a place
Where the lilacs grow
Kissed by the sun
Such a beautiful fragrance
Drifting on the breeze
Lush purple, sweet smell
Tickling the senses
Verdant are the flowers
That grow in your mind
Comforting memories of yesterday
Peaceful home standing in kindness
Sweet kisses from this place
Lilacs drifting on the breeze of
Yesterday

The Stars

I accept from the universe
all it wants to give me
so I can gather the stars.

I feel their light shine on me
twinkling a prism of color
falling on my head and shoulders
softly settling in my heart.
Today is a good day to be alive.

The Face of Fear

Today I read something that made me pause. It was the statement that when you have momentum the worst thing you can do is drop the ball. I know it is typical when you have written a book you feel, "I am done." and need to take time for a deserved rest. I felt a moment of anxiety, what does that mean for me? What should I be doing that maybe I am not doing? Should I feel guilty if I am doing nothing? And does that mean I am dropping the ball? Worry and guilt crept in. Then I remembered:

I am peace, kindness, passion, patience, wisdom, thankfulness and faith. I breathed a breath of release and knew I am in Divine harmony and momentum will happen in my life... Thank you.

The Hopeful Tree

This week my husband and I have taken off to recoup from months of grueling work on my mother's estate. We are camping. As I sit here and write I look up and see a huge old oak tree. The campground has cut off all the tree's limbs on one half to make room for the campers. The other half of the tree branches out to provide shade and a haven for birds and squirrels.

I can't help but to think the tree felt the chain saw cutting off its limbs. Did the person lopping off the limbs feel the tree's pain? What irony, I have gone to spend time in nature, only to see how we have callously destroyed part of the tree for our convenience.

The tree gives me hope. It is lopsided and brutalized but somehow it has survived. This tree has great energy and has done its job despite the trauma it has experienced. It is with a grateful heart I look at the tree and I will bask in its energy today.

Wintry Day

I watch out my window as the snow is slanting onto the ground. It is a silent day except for the sound of blowing wind; wet and wintry.

The snow collects on one side of the fencepost and attaches to the ground. Birds are hushed watching for the weather to let up so they can fly to my neighbor Frank's bird feeder. There is a hawk who hangs around the feeder to get easy prey, little devil. The squirrels, possums, and coyotes have all reached shelter until the weather lets up, but not the ducks. The ducks have been showing off today.

They flew in by the hundreds just before the snow and landed on the middle lake. We can hear them honking all hours of the day and night. How do they determine how many ducks are traveling together and how long they are staying? Nature has arranged their life. My life is being orchestrated too as I sit and watch winter out the window.

Writing

What I have to say about my writing is it centers and balances me. Writing is as creative as picking up a brush and painting a picture. It is a surprise, like enjoying opening a present at Christmas with anticipation. Writing is my friend; sometimes we laugh and sometimes we cry.

Don't Get Your Tit Caught in a Wringer

Sometimes memories pop into my head about my parents that make me laugh. I loved to listen to my Dad tell tales about his way of life when he was young. He was one of ten children, five boys and five girls. Life was tough for his family as his father died when he was eight years old. That didn't seem to hold my father down as you will notice in the story I am about to tell.

When my dad was young, his mother chose him to help with the laundry for the day. Wash day was an onerous chore for a family of eleven. Back then they had a washing machine that had rollers on it to wring out clothes. My dad was antsy.

He was mad and wanted to go outside to be with the boys. He kept whining to his mom to let him go but she stood firm. (She knew how to deal with ten youngsters.) Finally, in frustration my dad pulled up the end of his mom's apron and placed it in the roller's edge of the washer. When his mom turned on the roller, the machine turned into a monster dragged her closer and closer to being squished in it by the apron. She was in a panic as her tit was drawing close to being flattened like a pancake. Mom got the demon machine stopped and yelled at my dad,

"Go on, get out of here." My dad left on his way to be with his brothers with a smirk on his face.

I treasure this story because it captures the spirit of my dad. He:
* was a little spoiled being the youngest child
* was mischievous
* knew how to have fun
* was ingenious in working out problems and taking them to a resolution.

He carried all those characteristics through his mature life, and they made him charming. I hope I can remember this heritage as I go through life.

Life Is Too Short to Fold A Fitted Sheet

It's funny how life lessons come to you in strange ways. I have an awareness to receive them and I am working on being more mindful. That is hard for someone whose mind goes fifty miles an hour. That is just the point. I would like to share my mindfulness lesson for this week. My mother was a perfectionist, and she had a lock on being mindful before it was popular. When she did something, she did it right. Her powers of observation were keen. She corralled six kids without taking a breath. She always had a unique ability to be aware and listened to what people said. Whenever she did the most onerous job, she immersed herself and appreciated a job well done and loved to clean.

I remember one Christmas when all the family was together someone asked my Mom to show us how to fold a fitted sheet (Big family). She got up in front of all of us and whipped the sheet out and gave us a sheet folding lesson. When she finished that darned fitted sheet looked folded tidy and neat. It amazed us all. We had the most fun out of our sheet folding event.

What strikes me most was my Mom had unlimited energy and could do ten women's worth of work in a day. She took pleasure in every task she did and was bent on teaching us to, "do it the right way". (Ask her kids who had to wash dishes over again and again because she would find the littlest speck of dirt.) I wonder if she had such high energy because she was mindful. She didn't have time to worry about the past or future. Some days I am mindful and other days less so. I am a work in progress. "Life is too short to fold a fitted sheet," but I do it anyway because it is what my mom taught me. Here is a tribute to my mother. Thank you for your enthusiasm for life and all you have taught me.................

Ham & Beans

I remember my eighteenth birthday well. I was excited because I was traveling to Chicago to the Midwest Trade Show to learn all the latest hairstyles and techniques. The trade show boasted a convention center full of merchants with the latest products for styling hair. Famous hairstylists showed up to demonstrate latest the trend in hairstyling some of which I could take home for my clients. Some styles were so ridiculous I wouldn't have put them on my dog. Loud music blared everywhere; crowds were milling about with the latest clothes styles. The miniskirt barely covering the rear seemed to be the rage. I ran into the bathroom and hiked up my skirt at the waistband smiling to myself.

There was one booth with the newest products and tools on display. False eyelashes jumped out at me; I had never noticed them before. My imagination captured how sexy I would be as I wore them, I was eager to put them on. On the train ride home, I felt a thrill of happiness with my new false eyelashes tucked in my bag. What a treasure. I couldn't wait to go home and put them on for my husband Steve.

The first night I was home I cooked ham and beans for supper. In between the cooking I was in the bathroom putting on my new eyelashes to surprise Steve. They came with a glue that you put on the eyelashes and then you glued them to your eyes as well. What I didn't know was how hard it was to get the glue on the eyelash. I had to wait for the glue to dry on my eyes. Darn those eyelashes were hard to stick to my eyes. One side of the eyelash would stick down and the other would pop up. They were difficult to put on, my neck and face began to sweat. I was determined. Once the eyelashes were on, they were so long and heavy they beat my glasses. I could barely hold my eyes open. (Never mind, I will get used to them. No one told me you need to trim them.)

Fast forward. Steve was home, and it was dinner time. I have my sexy eyelashes on that I can't see out of. We sat at the table where the pot of ham and beans sat in the center. There was a bowl in front of Steve and me for the beans. I reached into the bean pot with a ladle and Steve held his bowl out for me to put the beans in. I can't see through the eyelashes. (I knew I was so sexy.) I ladled the beans into his bowl. Unfortunately, I missed the bowl and poured the beans on his hand. He looked up at me and said, "What the XXX!" I laughed uncontrollably.

To this day if we have ham and beans Steve looks expectantly at me and says, "Do you have your eyelashes on"? We both have a good laugh!

Homemade Donuts

There are big wet fluffy snowflakes coming down. It is beautiful to see them falling on the trees and water. They melt like cotton candy the minute they touch anything. Memories sneak in of my mother calling us to come over and have homemade donuts when it was snowing. Everyone in the family knew it was a tradition she did when it was wintry, cold and we were snowed in.

My husband and I, our daughter Stephanie and her husband bought my parents property when they passed away. Thirty-eight acres, a seven and half acre lake, a five-acre lake and smaller lake in the ravine behind our house. When mother owned the property, the grass was pristine like a mowed park. At eighty-three she maintained the property on her own and she could work circles around her kids. We are trying to live up to her standards which is not easy.

Stephanie and her husband live in mother's house. As I was thinking of my mom and homemade donuts Stephanie texted to ask if we would like to come for homemade donuts at six. I laugh at the synchronicity of her invite and my thoughts. She asked me if I had mom's recipe. I was sure I did but couldn't remember where it was. I found her a recipe that I thought was similar.

Stephanie was nervous about making the donuts. She had never made a recipe with yeast. Do you know how long you let the dough set? How do you knead the dough? What is the cooking time for the donuts? Interesting that mom decided to made donuts and, "Walla", donuts. Stephanie braved up and invited the neighbors Frank and Pati who have lived next to us as long as I can remember. Frank came from Germany and I know he doesn't eat sweets, but they said yes.

At six o'clock we arrived for donuts. Stephanie's German Shepherd (who is as big as me) greeted us at the door. He was running in circles in anticipation of visiting with my husband Steve. I saw him counter surfing trying to get donuts. They looked and smelled like my mom's. Yeast donuts have a yummy smell that make your mouth water. Stephanie's daughter was helping her by icing the finished donuts. Funny how smells bring back memories. One time when Steve was in Viet Nam, we mailed him a great big donut. He shared it with his fellow brothers. (I can't imagine how stale it was.) They thought they had died and gone to heaven.

I ate four darned donuts. Frank ate four of them and was proud of himself. That night I lay my head on my pillow (weighing five pounds more) and felt gratefulness that my daughter cared enough to carry a family tradition forward. Maybe I will make the donuts next time or not. Stephanie did a good job. She posted a picture of us eating her donuts for the rest of the family to see. I need not tell you all the comments. I could hear my mother telling me from heaven, "Stephanie pleases me".

Porky the Pig

I grew up on a working farm. We had hogs, cows, chickens, ducks; all needing to eat and drink water. My siblings and I knew the reality of farm life. All those animals were chores for us six kids. You eat what you raise so don't get attached to the animals. There was eleven years difference between myself as the oldest and my youngest sister Nancy. As adults, my sister Nancy and Deborah tell me they can't remember a time when my husband Steve wasn't in their lives. My childhood memories differ from my younger sisters Debbie and Nancy but we all can remember Porky the pig.

Dad came in from the barn holding a newborn pig. He told us the piglet was the runt of the litter and his siblings wouldn't let him eat. The tiny pig had our sympathy right away. He wanted to know if we would take turns bottle feeding him so he would live. We promptly named the little bitty pig Porky. Porky was pink, soft as velvet and settled in our arms immediately. He looked at us as his squinty eyes rolled back in his head in delight. He took up residence in a box in the living room.

We kids often argued over whose turn it was to feed the pig. We talked and cooed at Porky while we fed him. Porky grew and flourished. My younger sisters Nancy and Debbie used to dress Porky up in clothes and pink bonnet to pull him around in a little red wagon. The little pig fit in it perfectly. He would look up at the sisters with his adorable little eyes and he knew they loved him. Porky thought at that moment maybe he was a girl human.

Porky grew too big for the wagon in time. He followed us on his short legs around the house all the time. Mom drew the line at him sleeping with us. She made him go back to the box, but the box was soon getting too small. We had to trade it in on a bigger model. Porky wondered if he was a dog. He saw the German Shepherd following everyone around and knew they were a man's best friend. He was our best friend.

Porky would go explore and later come back to us kids to plop down next to us with a grunt. We would talk to him, scratch his back and neck, and tickle his ears. His eyes would roll up in his skull and he would make a delighted snort when we did that.

Dad finally made a dreaded announcement that we knew was coming. Porky had to move out in the hog lot with the other pigs. We protested to no avail. Dad stood resolute; he was a farmer. Out Porky went to the hog lot.

Porky took one peek at the big hogs and he turned around to go back home. Boars and sows were scary looking and were glaring at him. All of them stuck their snouts in slop and grunted while they ate. What was that sickening smell? Pew!! How disgusting. The pigs had one look at Porky and determined he didn't belong. He was too clean.

Porky so missed his people. He was homesick. Soon Porky squeezed through the fence and went back home. He was returning to where the kids loved him. The children saw him and tried to hide him. Ha! Except his oinking noises of delight gave him away. Dad grabbed Porky and took him right back to the pig lot. It turned out there was no fence that could separate Porky from his family. He still didn't know how he fit in, but he was not a pig!

My new boyfriend Steve came to the farm to go hunting with my Dad one day. Steve liked the farm (and me a little) because he was always seeing something new. My Dad and Steve climbed over the fence and walked to the back pasture when Porky decided maybe he was a hunting dog. He squirmed between the fence and ran on his squatty legs to catch up oinking all the way. Porky was as excited as Steve to go hunting.

When Porky finally caught up with Steve and Dad he was out of breath. He was rustling the grass with his short legs and making all kinds of noise. Dad was irritated because he would scare off the quail. My dad turned around and yelled to Porky, "go home"! My Dad was staring down Porky and Porky was staring back. I could have told Porky it was dangerous to defy Dad. Each of us kids learned our loving Dad could give a superhuman spanking for willful defiance of his orders.

Dad was generous and gave a second warning, again saying, "Porky, I said go home!" Porky stood his ground with stubbornness staring down Dad. Since Steve was closer to Porky my dad said to Steve, "Kick him." Steve looked at Dad in surprise and took a half-hearted kick with his foot and grazed Porky. Porky still didn't move. Dad stepped around Steve and kicked Porky in the snout hard enough it hurt so he got the message. Dad was boss. OOH that hurt! Porky turned around running back up the trail making oinking noises all the way. Dad had wounded his snout and pride.

Porky sat on the steps pouting. That was mean of Dad!

I came out the front door and there was Porky. He looked like his nose was out of joint over something. I could have sworn he was pouting. I sat down next to him and scratched his back and tickled his ears. He got out of his funk and gave me a sweet oink. Porky had decided he did not want to be a hunting dog.

Back to the pig lot for Porky, but it seemed Porky might have been Houdini. Porky was big by this time, in his teenage years by pig age. Still not one fence could keep him in.

Dad had plopped Porky in the hog lot again. Porky looked around in disdain and then he spied a new pig that had arrived from the auction house. Wow! He locked eyes with the pretty pig across the hog lot and it was love at first sight. His heart was beating fast; he caught his breath as he looked at the girl pig. Her beady eyes were beautiful. She had the prettiest snout he had ever seen and pink luscious lips. Porky dove into the mud and covered himself from head to toe. Just for good luck he took a second dive to make sure he smelled foul. He came up out of the mud. He held his breath as his eyes locked with hers. She oinked giving him a look; he oinked.

Maybe I am a male pig...

The Old Oak Tree

I grew up on a farm most of my life and I thought it was an inspiring place to live. I was the oldest of six children. Many times, we would pack a lunch and go to the timber for the day. We always had a special destination and that day the trip was to the old oak tree.

We had a pet pig that followed us most of the way until he lost interest. He turned around because it was too far for him and he went oinking home. We walked along the creek looking for cool rocks and feathers, following the trail to the old oak tree. I mean this was "THE TREE".

We had to climb in between an electric fence to get to the pasture with the tree. More than one of us got burned crawling in between the barbed wire. Ouch! Still it was worth it.

Our excitement increased as we got closer to the tree and finally arrived. We looked up in amazement at the old oak tree and our heart's beat faster. The ancient oak tree had branches that swung to the ground to welcome us. This tree had experienced life. All of us kids heard the tree welcoming us and whispering, "I am so happy to see you." Its tree limbs shuttered and bent down to greet us. Leaves glistened in the sun.

The energy the old oak tree gave out was extraordinary. Nothing was as exhilarating as scaling the limbs, swinging with our heads down like a monkey and then rotating up to land on top of the branch. The view over the tops of the trees was breath-taking. Birds hopped limb to limb and squirrels all scattered. We played all day pretending to be queens and kings. Our imaginations never ran out.

I have been back to visit the old oak tree two times since I have been an adult. Once with my youngest sister. When we came up to the tree my sister wrapped her arms around the trunk of the tree and she said she heard a whisper, "Where have you been?"

Fifty years later I traveled back to see the tree and had difficulty locating it.

The forest had grown up around the tree squeezing it into littleness. I felt its sadness at not being special anymore. Truth of the matter is the old oak tree is still extraordinary. It will always be a special place in six kids' hearts, etched in their memories.

Our Old Oak Tree

The old oak tree, I wonder what tales it could tell,
Of Kings and Queens, and fairies' dwell,
Children laughing, bending with the limbs,
Swinging, drinking of that dark oak well,
Daydreams of fairy streams and whims.
And dreams imagined
Too strange to tell.
Children's magic, light hearts and fun,
Breeze blowing their hair in the sun
As they climb from limb to limb.
Picnic lunches and tea-time on a whim
While the sun glistens through the leaves,
Shining on their shirts and sleeves,
The old oak tree smiles at their fun,
A haven for their pranks each one,
Too strange to tell.

Time has passed at long last,
Yet the old oak tree stands tall and proud,
Somewhat lonely without all the crowd.
The wind does yet whisper if you listen

It will tell.
Of a tale of children's laughing, fairies,
Queens and kings, swinging in the breeze.
I can hear the old oak tree calling me,
Memories I love so well,

Children's' laughter of glee
Of my sisters and brothers one,
All now grown, memories of the fun
Children have they of all their own.
Kings and queens, they have known
Perhaps someday their kids can find
Trees and children twined
The old oak tree and hear
Our voices with the wind to endear

Of the stories it must tell.
And tell its lonely limbs a kind word,
Of long-ago time heard.

Let it know it served so well,
Memories, laughter and fun do tell
Tree and children one,
Oh, what memories and fun
That old oak tree would tell.

Uncle Everette

Old people's smell bombarded me as I walked into the house. Have you ever had to do something as a kid you didn't want to do? Several times a year my mother loaded six of us children in the station wagon and we traveled to her Uncle Everette's house to clean. One time I was cleaning the kitchen and the sugar canister had maggots in it. I was guilty of throwing his kitchen stove knobs down the toilet with the pail of cleaning water but that didn't get me off the hook. Too bad, my mom reminded me to pick up the broom and clean!

Uncle Everette, tall and skinny, had a long beard that tickled his chest. His intelligent blue eyes pierced my heart as I understood he was a prophet in disguise. Uncle Everette was smart, and I admired him. Aunt Oreta was a dainty wife and schoolteacher who had taught Uncle Everette to read when he was thirty.

Uncle Everette was not immune to life challenges. He had one leg that was longer than the other because of a failed surgery. When you went into his bedroom, a long rope hung from the ceiling which he used to get out of bed. His disabilities didn't seem to hold him down. He approached them without complaint.

My mother looked after Uncle Everette in his later life years. I had to laugh sometimes because he was tight with his money. He would ask my mother to go to the post office and get him stamps giving her enough money for one stamp. His house was bare by today's standards, material possessions did not matter to him. What did matter to him was God and his Bible.

When Uncle Everette turned ninety-one I took my camera to his house. I photographed him in his rocking chair with the sunlight beaming on him with his bible in the palms of his hands. It is a remarkable photograph as different hanging on the wall, as he was in person. I am reminded that small times you spend with people can have big influences on them. When I see the picture hanging on the wall, I wonder what small ways I am influencing others. We often become lost chasing after the big dreams trying to make a difference when all we need be is who we are. Today I have a reminder that simple actions and deeds can produce a difference. Thank you, Uncle Everette for having the courage to be different.

More precious that money are the bible stories he taught me and the positive influence of knowing a man that loves God. The image of Uncle Everette sitting in his rocking chair, barefooted, beard hitting his chest, sun shining on his face will be in my heart forever.

Washtub Soup

Have you ever heard of washtub soup? I doubt it. It was a special menu for my family on the weekends.

When I was a kid, we used to have lots of company on Saturday and Sunday. My father came from a family of ten kids and my mother from a family of six. My father's and mother's siblings had four or five kids themselves. We had lots of extended family. I loved it because I had lots of cousins to play with. There were about ten of us close in age.

On the weekend company would converge on us. The uncles

came to hunt rabbits, squirrels or deer depending on what season it was. Sometimes the adults would play pinochle or rummy. While the uncles were hunting us kids would play and play until lunch time. Around ten o'clock they put us to work peeling vegetables, lots of vegetables for home-made vegetable soup.

They then threw all the vegetables into a washtub that mom kept for making homemade vegetable soup.

I must laugh because the first time my husband Steve came to our house there was a washtub of soup cooking on the stove. He thought mom was cleaning our socks. Boy was he in for a surprise. My mom made homemade bread to go along with the soup. I loved to watch the bread poof up and then she punched it down. Sometimes she would let us help make the rolls. The raw dough smelled like yeast and was like elastic. Biting into those baked buttery rolls was delicious; the hotter the better. If we were lucky mom had made pies to go with the soup and rolls. After lunch we would all just lounge around too full to do anything until it was time to do the dishes. Guess who the dish washers were. Us kids. We would stand at the sink for what seemed like hours washing dishes. To make matters worse, if you left a spot on them Mom pounced on the dish and made you wash it again. I hated washing dishes then, and I hate washing dishes now.

What was so special about those memories was security and family went hand in hand. When my Mom and Dad celebrated their fiftieth anniversary all of us kids threw my Mom and Dad a surprise party.

We sent out the invitations laughing. On the menu was homemade washtub vegetable soup and rolls. The guest chuckled and enjoyed memories of hunting, home and soup.

Times have changed. Everyone is too busy to visit with family. We purchase food at Kentucky Fried Chicken or McDonald's. Many of the family members have now passed away, and no one comes to hunt.

Meditations and Chants

Meditation on Spirit
Beverly Arnold Oberline

Wolf Spirit Energy
7.15.19

As we begin our journey to welcome Spirit, imagine walking along a path. You are in the high desert, walking on dusty sandstone, very smooth from all the feet which have trod it over the centuries. The day is warm and the sun is bright, warming the reddish boulders which appear alongside the path. There is a beautiful cool breeze which you can hear sighing through the ancient cottonwood trees and wafting the scent of pinion pine to your nostrils. The way is smooth and winds through the trees and rocks and the air is pleasant.

As you continue walking, you notice that you can hear water ahead. You can hear it splashing on rocks, gurgling and chuckling, and as you round a curve past a large boulder, the path begins to slope downward toward a clear and beautiful stream. Just near the edge is an old, old cottonwood tree. It has huge roots and between two of the largest, time and erosion have created a perfect place to sit. As you do so, you notice it is cushioned with pine needles and shaded by the graceful old tree above. It is near enough you can feel the coolness of the water, but still dry, and the tree's roots act as comfortable arm rests.

As you relax in your warm and well-padded seat, I want you to think of your body as sacred space in living flesh. We contain all the physical elements: we are made of mostly water but we also contain myriad chemicals, metals and matter which are of the earth. We breathe in oxygen and breathe out carbon dioxide in a mutual working with the trees, and the electrical impulses in our hearts and our brains are no less than the same fire that lights the sun and the stars. It is into this sacred space you will invite Spirit. It represents our place of groundedness as well as our connection to the highest part of ourselves, the divinity within us and opens us to the cosmic consciousness – in whatever way you may define that. There is no right or wrong definition. Spirit and belief are as individual to each of us as our fingerprints. However, you define Spirit is how it works for you.

Now I want you to open your root chakra. Feel the energy, the warmth of the Earth come up through the stone you are sitting on. Allow that energy and opening to move up through the sacral chakra and into your heart chakra. Imagine and feel your heart opening, expanding, growing wider until you feel that energy throughout your body, every cell where your heart pumps blood. Now move to your throat chakra, that place of true speaking, then up to your intuitive third eye, and now open your crown.

For a moment, just feel yourself open to the universal energy, open and pulsating with life, and in that openness, now, ask Spirit to join you and Spirit will answer.

As you begin your communication with Spirit, feel all the open places now suffused with light as well as life. Feel the warmth and the brightness of the light as it comes now through your crown and down through your body to create an infinity loop of never ending, always living, always being, golden light.

Just sit with Spirit for a bit and become comfortable knowing and recognizing each other. Spirit will always be with us. It is we who have to recognize the Spirit within ourselves. You may, or may not, receive a message from Spirit at this time. You may want to ask a question. You may get a direct answer, or just experience a kind of knowing. There may be no direct communication at all, just the feeling of connection, a joining to All That Is, knowing you are a part of everything, and everything is a part of you. Again, there is no right or wrong. Spirit is real though ethereal; it will reveal itself in many guises and it is up to us to recognize when Spirit is giving us information.

With the connection to Spirit and to All That Is, acknowledge and understand that you have everything you will ever need contained inside the sacred space that is your Self. Spirit will be with you and will answer when called upon.

As you rise from your pleasant seat, and begin to walk up the slope, take a moment for a deep breath.

Continuing up the gentle slope we find our way again, past the large boulder now warm from the sun. Take another deep breath and begin to return to now.

Walking now on the dusty sandstone, breathing in and out, coming closer to consciousness with each exhale.

And when you are ready, open your eyes.

Seasonal Chants
Jean Hembrough

SEASONAL CHANTS – INTRODUCTION

What is the difference between poems and chants? That is a difficult question to answer definitively for several reasons. First, there are a great variety of styles within each of these genres by themselves. Second, the demarcation lines between these two genres are often porous. Third, some of the definition for each genre is subjective to the authors' and readers' personal perspectives. Having said all of that, the following five works are offered as chants. The intention of the author is that they be read and experienced with rhythms as if they are being accompanied by drums. No specific rhythmic direction for any of the chants is given other than dashes and spaces to indicate how the author felt the beat as she wrote. The reader should feel free to experiment with whatever beats she or he feels may fit the chants in their own experience.

-- Jean Hembrough, 11 May 2019

SEASONS

Seasons come - - - seasons go
Ride the tides - - - go with flow.
Summer, autumn - - - winter, spring;
Treasure each new - - - gift they bring.
Seasons come - - - seasons go.
Where they'll take us - - - we don't know.
Seasons come - - - seasons go.
Ride the tides - - - go with flow.

-- 20 March 2019

SEASONS - AUTUMN

Welcome - - Lady Autumn.
Bring your - - colors bright.
Welcome - - Lady Autumn.

Farewell - - waning light.
Fruit and - - grain are ripe now.
Gather - - all within.
Grateful - - for each blessing,
Dance and - - chant begin.
Let the - - bonfires beckon.
Stories - - now are told.
Welcome - - Lady Autumn.
Turn our year - - from young to old.

-- 29 March 2019

SEASONS - SPRING

Springtime warmth begins to grow,
Melting lingering winter snow.
With drum and chant for Mother Earth,
We help her bring new life to birth.
Welcome flowers, buds, and grass.
Let cold and darkness fade and pass.
The time is come for life anew.
Thank you, Mother. Praise to you.

-- 13 March 2019

SEASONS - SUMMER

The wheel has brought us summer's heat.
We bless the earth with dancing feet.
We bless the sky with drum and song.
Mother's life in us is strong.
We join in circles far and near.
Together banish every fear.
Proclaim we now the way of light.
Feel our power. Share our sight.
The wheel has brought us summer days.
May peace be found in all our ways.

-- 11 April 2019

SEASONS - WINTER

Rest beneath the deep'ning snow.
Fear not as the winds now blow,
Bringing cold and frosty ways
To long nights and short, grey days.
Winter's time has come at last.
Another cycled year is past.
Draw we close to hearth and kin.
Let the fallow time begin.
Mother Nature, now at rest,
Welcomes all unto her breast
Where she cradles, softly sings
Till again we welcome spring.
Rest beneath the deep'ning snow.
Fear not as the cold winds blow.

-- 30 March 2019

Excerpts from Larger Work:

An Excerpt from READING SYMBOLIC SIGNS

How to Connect the Dots of Your Spiritual Life
By Jean Ferratier

An Orb: Is It a Dot?

I am intrigued by orbs. I can't help it. My camera goes everywhere I go. It is a device that helps me view things that my naked eye cannot. Orbs are spheres of light ranging from dense to translucent, mostly white but occasionally colored that appear on digital flash photography. I scrutinize every photo I see looking for orbs, noticing brightness, amount, size, shape, and placement. Orbs can appear in photographs around breathing physical forms such as people, animals, and nature. But what a surprise! They also appear in pictures with inanimate (non- breathing) objects, such as houses, furniture, walls or any solid matter.

People ask me, "Why do you think orbs are a sign?" When I see orbs in my photographs, I feel like I am given the blessings of a tangible sign that there are miracles all around me. I am filled with awe every time orbs appear. Looking at hundreds of pictures of orbs convinces me that there are wonderful Light Beings that are beyond our normal spectrum of vision. I view them as Angels and Spirit Guides that are evidence of guidance and support from the Universal Divine.

Some might ask, "Is it dust?" "Is my camera defective?" I even noted that my camera directions notated that "spots" might occur. The directions did not account for these "spots" having common characteristics of a defined nucleus, and an appearance of a pattern within it. The questions and explorations are boundless. If you are a bit of a pioneer and visionary, then wondering what message orbs carry for you can be a new frontier, as it is for me.

~Connect the Dots~

~You might want to review your photos. Do you see any orbs? If not, don't worry, I am available to help you successfully see orbs in photos and take orb pictures. Usually once orbs are shown to you, you will find them easily in pictures.~

Excerpts from "Restorative Yoga"

Nancy Hodge Long

YOGA
is available
to everyone. Yoga is
the practice of non-striving.
It is accepting yourself, letting go into your
natural flow. The breath is used to help find your
flow and to connect your body, mind and spirit.
Yoga is not about doing, but rather being.
Being in the present moment and
allowing the body/mind to
deeply feel each
sensation.

‒ ‒ ‒ ‒ ‒ ‒ ‒ ‒ ‒ ‒

To truly relax is to simply be…
Restorative poses support and bring balance,
allowing the body/mind to move into its natural healing process.

‒ ‒ ‒ ‒ ‒ ‒ ‒ ‒ ‒ ‒

When you find a position
so comfortable that your body is light and open
and your breath is soft and quiet,
you have reached an experiential understanding of
Restorative Yoga.

You have made the practice your own.
You no "do"
but rather simply
"be."

‒ ‒ ‒ ‒ ‒ ‒ ‒ ‒ ‒ ‒

Watching the breath
is the way to focus on the present moment.
Begin by inhaling through the
nostrils and felling the sensation of air inside the body.

Let the belly fill with breath. Notice all of the
sensations. Move deep inside and fell each sensation.
Your body will know to exhale.
Follow the flow of breath all the way out
of your body. Feel how
empty the space
inside your body
is.

_ _ _ _ _ _ _ _ _ _

Life
brings cycles
of activity and rest.

We need both
to find balance,
health and well-being.

Rest
brings a time to
renew, restore, and rejuvenate.

_ _ _ _ _ _ _ _ _ _

Breathing
into the back body
brings attention to an often ignored
part of the body.

Yogis
believe the ego
is associated with the front of the body
while your deeper true nature is
found in the back body.

_ _ _ _ _ _ _ _ _ _

Breath is life.
Yoga
tells us
we are each given

a finite number of breaths for our lifetime.
When you deepen and lengthen your breath, you extend your
lifespan by not using your breaths as quickly.

Restorative poses
Help you increase your lung capacity.
The respiratory system opens and your lungs accept more breath.
These poses, practiced regularly,
help develop the ability
to let go and
just BE.

— — — — — — — — — —

Look within and find what you love.
Give yourself
the only gift you truly can,
Awareness
in each moment.

— — — — — — — — — —

Let your practice unfold from inside.
Think of it as a silk thread, smooth and strong.
Let it connect you to the stillness found within.

— — — — — — — — — —

Ahh~
Shavasana brings absolute rest.
It is a symbolic dying to all distractions~ inner and outer. It offers
stillness.

And in stillness resides.
All That Is.

Excerpts from My Golden Heart; Putting the Pieces Back Together Again

Sharron Magyar

The Eagle Meditation

Always do meditation in a relaxing, private place. You may tape record this meditation and play it back.

Take a deep breath. Inhale deeply into your belly for seven counts; hold your breath for seven counts; exhale for seven counts and hold for seven counts. Repeat this process seven times. Breathe in tranquility and peace as you inhale. Breathe out stress and tension as you exhale. Eventually, you will step into a natural breathing rhythm and fall into a deep relaxation.

Imagine you see the eagle sweep down and land. You climb up on his back. He rises into the air, higher and higher into the sky. You feel the wind against your face and the sun soaking into your skin. Stress leaves your body.

The more you soar upon the wind, the freer you become of all worries and strain. You look down upon the earth and you become connected with the universe. You realize those things you spend your days worrying about are really nothing except your imagination at play.

You breathe the air into your body and hold it deep in your belly. Then you exhale, and with each out breath you exhale stress. You are free!

When your body has released all stress, you and your eagle return to the earth. You breathe peace into your body. When you have returned home you count to five and open your eyes to reorient into the room

Energy Exchange Meditation

Always do meditation in a relaxing, private place. You may tape record this meditation and play it back.

Take a deep breath. Inhale deeply into your belly for seven counts; hold your breath for seven counts; exhale for seven counts and hold for seven counts. Repeat this process seven times.

Focus on releasing all negativity while exhaling. Breathe in tranquility and peace as you inhale. Breathe out stress and tension as you exhale. You will step into a natural breathing rhythm and fall into a deep relaxation.

When relaxed practice imagining energy exchanges in your relationships to find the imbalances. Are you giving too much energy, are you taking too much energy, or is there an equal exchange of energy?

If you are the one who constantly gives energy, the result can be burnout and an overwhelmed feeling. If you allow others to always take your energy, it can take a toll on your self-esteem and cause reduced or depleted energy. If you are a taker of energy, you've set yourself up for loneliness.

In your mind, imagine an equal exchange of energy between you and each of your relationships. Noticing your energy is pivotal to personal transformation.

Practice this exercise every night before sleeping until you step into a more appropriate energy exchange in your relationships. When you feel the process is completed, breathe deeply, and count to five, then bring your awareness back to the room. (Warning: Sometimes you may have to let go of a relationship if they continually take your energy.)

Sunflower Meditation
(for people who have suffered trauma)

You can read it to someone at night right before they go to sleep or record and listen to it with headphones or earbuds.

Once upon a time, there grew a very special sunflower. It was a sunflower that started to grow on very solid ground. But the wind and the rains came after it started growing, blowing it this way and that. The wind and rain were strong, unpredictable, and scary.

The flower became all mixed up about who it was and how it was supposed to grow. Rather than growing into a tall solid sunflower, it split into many different flowers, each different in maturity, age, and size. Somehow the flower split to protect itself against the storms. One part became a flower growing tall and skinny; another part of the flower was bending over, its leaves hanging low in sorrow. A third flower was like a rose filled with thorns, prickly and hurt from the split. A very young sprout grew out of the flower with a very diseased leaf, and an old hard seed.

The sunflower could not grow in the way it was intended to grow, because it was split into many different individual flowers. Parts of it were tall, parts of it were small, but it was all mixed up. The other sunflowers in the garden did not understand this sunflower at all, because they had never seen a sunflower like it before. They often snickered and made fun of the sunflower because it was different.

One day, a fairy came walking through the flower garden, and stopped before the confused sunflower. The fairy got a very puzzled look on her face and said, "Gosh little flower, you somehow have gotten all mixed up. You're supposed to be a sunflower, but you have split into many different flowers. And that means you can't grow tall and straight and beautiful to feel the warmth of the sun."

The little sunflower started to cry, and the fairy was taken aback, because she didn't know sun flowers could cry. The flower sobbed, "I know I'm all mixed up." She felt terrible. The flower told the fairy, "The winds and the rains hurt me when I was little." Sometimes one part of me doesn't know what the other part is doing, and I feel confused. The sunflower asked the fairy to help her.

The fairy looked at the sunflower intensely, and then decided that maybe she had a solution. She said, "I must cut away the leaves of all the different flowers that grow from your stem. Then I'll wrap you up, so you grow into one strong healthy stem."

"How bad will it hurt me?" asked the sunflower as she was crying.

The fairy said, "It might hurt a little bit, but after it's done you will feel much, much prettier and stronger." The little sunflower was afraid but decided she would not let her fear keeps her from growing as it had before. As carefully as she could, the fairy stripped off the funny looking leaves and then separated the stems, which grew from the sunflower. Then the fairy wrapped some silk from the spider around the flower, making sure, that all the stems were close together. The fairy reassured the sunflower, "I'll be back later to take away the silk. You may soon find you are one solid sunflower again."

The sunflower felt a little strange and scared but she grew stronger and healed more and more. Sometimes, for a moment, she was sorry that she'd met the fairy, especially when she saw that it was going to rain, and the wind was going to blow, but she wasn't unhappy for very long. Mostly, she was encouraged that all her parts could grow together as the fairy had predicted.

Before long, the fairy was back, "I'm going to remove the silk," the fairy informed the flower. Let's look at you." The sunflower was happy to discover her stem was now solid, although her leaves were a little pale yellow from being covered up. This made the sunflower frightened. The fairy saw her anxiety.

"Your leaves will be healthy as soon as the sun shines on them," said the fairy. "Soon you will be completely healed, and no one will remember that you were anything other than a beautiful sun flower."
The sunflower cried tears of joy, she was so delighted. "How can I thank you?" she asked.

"You can thank me by growing stronger and stronger every day. You will be the sturdiest sunflower in the garden." The sunflower grew; she flourished, standing straight and tall to shine in the sun. The fairy danced away smiling; she knew the sunflower was going to be alright.

Memoirs
from Don O'Neal

A Little Knowledge...

Agriculture was among my favorite high-school classes, because of its wide variety of activities, such as building hog houses, developing grass water-ways, participated in debates, and judging livestock, to name just a few.

For me, judging livestock was one of the most interesting, as we learned to assess the finer points that would make the difference between championship animals and those that were just ordinary. We spent a lot of time on various local farms, practicing how to judge beef cattle, hogs, sheep, and dairy cows, and while we were becoming more familiar with the process, our teacher, Mr. Riley, was evaluating our individual judging abilities.

Occasionally we would participate in livestock judging contests, usually sponsored by 4H or FFA (Future Farmers of America,) where Riley would divide us up into judging teams, one for each of the different types of livestock. Although I raised hogs as a project, I was never very good at judging them, or any of the other livestock classes for that matter. But he encouraged me to participate anyway, and I enjoyed it.

One year a group of us went to the University of Illinois for the State FFA Convention, which featured one of the most prestigious livestock judging contests. Based on our individual judging experience up to that point, Riley assigned each of us to one of the four-member teams. Those who were best at beef cattle were assigned to that category, and so on.

After he had appointed the four major teams, beef cattle, dairy cattle, hogs, and sheep, three of us were left over; those who weren't very good at any of the major judging classes. On the morning of the judging, as Riley drove the school bus to drop each team at its judging area, those of us who hadn't made any of the teams were thinking maybe we'd have the day free to explore the campus. But we should have known better. After dropping off the last team, Riley got back on the school bus and informed the rest of us that we were now his chicken-judging team.

Chicken-judging? None of us had ever judged chickens and didn't know the first thing about it. But Riley shrugged off our protests and, as he drove us to the chicken-judging area, gave us a quick overview of how to judge chickens. The only part of his advice I remember was that it had to do with the color of their beaks and feet.

Livestock judging involved several pens, each containing four animals or, in our case, birds. A team's challenge was to rank-order the birds in each pen, trying to match what the judges had already determined as their ideal rankings. In other words, the team was to decide, for each pen, which bird we thought was best, which was second best, and so on. The best possible score for a pen was when a team's 1, 2, 3, and 4 rankings matched the rankings that had been pre-determine by the judges. The second-best score was when a team had the best bird ranked number 1 and the worst ranked number 4, but the middle two birds reversed. For example, the 2nd best bird ranked number 3 and the 3rd best ranked number 2. For anything less than that, the scores dropped
off dramatically.

Riley left us there and went back to watch the other teams do their judging, saying he'd pick us up later, after he had picked up the other teams. As unprepared as we felt, we went about our business, basing our judgment entirely on Riley's rules of thumb, primarily the colors of the birds' beaks and feet. As you might imagine, we were more than a little intimidated by the other teams' apparent knowledge in what they were doing. They seemed to be considering a lot more than just beak and foot color. But we did our best, and waited for the results.

When Riley picked us up a few hours later, we learned that our first- place ribbon was the only ribbon that had been earned by any of our school's teams!

The moral of the story? Sometimes a little knowledge is better than too much, (or is it "Ignorance is bliss?")

Before the Memories Fade

The small-town barbershop is gradually becoming just a memory, of a part of life that was unique, interesting, and always entertaining. Mike's, for example, was a one-chair shop that didn't offer hair styling, manicures, or even appointments, yet for years I drove more than 20 miles to have my hair cut, although there were dozens of barbers much closer to home. Why? In no small part because "no appointments" meant there was always a small group of customers waiting their turn, and their conversations, alone, were worth the trip. Here's how I remember a typical visit.

Mike was the shop's proprietor, and its only barber, and for more than 50 years he had worked from 8:00 AM until 6:00 PM with no lunch break, although during his 70s he had cut back to three days a week, in an attempt at gradual retirement.

When I walk in there are three people ahead of me - one in the barber chair, and two waiting. I greet Mike, sit down and pick up one of an assortment of hunting, fishing, and automobile magazines, not so much to read but to use as a prop; something to hold while I observe what's going on, and eavesdrop on the ongoing conversations. Mike is a great story teller, and his customers-in-waiting are an ever-changing cast of characters, with an unlimited range of interests and "expertise."

I glance at the shop's bulletin board, which features a hand-lettered "No Profanity, Please" sign, to see what's going on in the community, and what new cartoons or sale notices may have been added since my last visit. The shop is small, perhaps fifteen by twenty feet, with one barber chair and 6 well-worn wooden arm chairs. On his window sill is an assortment of puzzles; not crosswords, or picture puzzles, but the type that challenge you to take apart two pieces of metal that have been twisted together in a seemingly inseparable manner. In the spring some of the puzzles get shoved aside to make room for the tomato-plant seedlings he'll be starting for his garden.

Nobody seems to mind that the shop doesn't have a television or a radio, so the only sounds, besides the buzzing of Mike's clippers and the snipping of his scissors, are conversations; often several going on at the same time. By listening carefully, you can be privy to advice on almost any topic, like how to keep aphids off your roses, or the best way to filet a crappie. And I learn about a lot of other things that I had no idea would interest me, such as how the high school football team is looking this year, or what kind of corn yields local farmers are getting.

A faint smell of left-over smoke suggests that the fellow sitting next to me hasn't yet kicked the habit, although Mike did years ago, and no longer allows smoking in his shop. But my favorite aroma is the subtle, slightly sweet smell of bay rum. You might say it's the background scent of the barbershop, and it will linger for quite

---

a while after I leave, as a reminder of where I've been, for me and anyone who might get close to me during the rest of the day.

When it's my turn in the chair, my perspective changes somewhat, for now I'm in the center of the action, and feel as though I'm the focal point of all the conversations. But instead of joining in, I just sit back to enjoy the comfort of having my hair cut and neck shaved, by someone who has, over the years, become as much a friend as my barber. Mike's touch is that of a master craftsman, as he deftly wields the sharpest straight-razor you can imagine, making it glide across my skin like a gentle massage.

I settle in, close my eyes, and am half-listening to one discussion about how to preserve peppers so they keep their taste without losing their firmness, and another about canning green tomatoes, when I suddenly realize my mouth is watering, because, you see, a trip to the barber wasn't just for tonsorial maintenance; it was always an educational experience, and sometimes a treat for all the senses.

WHY COMPETITION?

A popular belief is that the success of an organization depends on how effective it is in out-competing other organizations. And we are led to believe that the same is true for people; that our personal success depends on how well we compete against other people. Although competition among organizations may be necessary, the same is not true for individuals.

Competition among people is not necessary, and only exists because of the way individual performance is measured.

Competition in Schools

In his book, No Contest: The Case Against Competition. Alfie Kohn tells us, "...our schooling, from the earliest grades, trains us not only to triumph over others but to regard them as obstacles to our own success." (1986:2) In other words, we teach our children that in order to succeed in school they must strive to be better than those around them, and that philosophy seems to drive education at all levels, from elementary school through college.

Student performance is usually measured by some form of grading (e.g., A,B,C,) and most institutions grade on some sort of curve, where only a small percentage of students (e.g., 10-20%) are allowed to achieve A's and B's, while the rest get lower grades.

That puts students in competition with one another for the few high grades that are available. It's an approach that seems to be favored by administrators, who worry that giving more than just a few A's would be seen as "grade inflation" and shouldn't be allowed.

So students are forced into a "me versus them" mindset which constantly reminds them that anyone else who gets an A decreases their chance of getting one, and automatically puts students in a competition where a few become "winners" and the rest have to settle for lower grades. But we could eliminate that kind of competition and give every student the opportunity for a good grade by doing away with the curve and grading all students against a common standard. Then students would only be competing against themselves as they try to improve their grades, but not at anyone else's expense. In that kind of environment, students learn more, are more likely to enjoy the learning experience, and are more willing to work with other students instead of against them.

Competition in Organizations

Just like schools, most organizations put their employees in competition with one another. It may not always be intentional, but it is pervasive. At lower levels in an organization competition is likely to be largely through peer pressure and be relatively invisible. Like when a new employee works harder than his associates as he tries to make a good first impression, and they warn him, "Slow down, you're making the rest of us look bad."

At higher organization levels, competition is more intense and more visible, as some employees feel they must compete hard for the next promotion. But at any level, that degree of competition only exists when individual performance is measured on a curve.

Evaluating Performance

A critical element of performance evaluation, often overlooked, is how we measure success.

Students' success, for example, is usually measured by their knowledge of a particular subject -- the quantity and quality of what they know of the subject matter. In like manner, employee success is measured by output -- the quantity and quality of what was accomplished of the assigned task.

Another important element of success, but one that is more difficult to measure, is performance improvement. While improvement can be measured by pre- and post-testing, putting a grade on it is not so easy. So perhaps the best way to address it is by convincing students and employees that continuous improvement is essential to keeping up in a constantly changing world, where improvement brings its own rewards. A student who enters a course with some knowledge of the subject matter should have an easier time reaching the required level of knowledge than one who enters with little or no knowledge. The student with no knowledge will need to work hard to earn an A, while the one with inherent knowledge may be able to coast the entire semester and still earn an A.

So the student with little knowledge has a strong incentive to improve, because his grade depends on it. But what incentive does the student with pre-knowledge have to put forth more than just minimal effort, if he can earn an A without it? None at all, unless you consider that by earning an A by doing less than his best, he's liable to get the impression he can coast through life believing there's no need to ever do more than the minimum required. And that's a sure-fire formula for how a winner can ultimately become a loser.

And the same applies to an employee who, due to her inherent knowledge and skills, finds it easier to reach a high level of performance than one who starts out with minimal knowledge or skills. What incentive will she have to put forth more than just minimal effort, and what will keep her from coasting through life believing there's no need to ever do more than the minimum required?

But if we can convince people of the value of continuous improvement no matter how good they are now, those who begin with fewer assets can become good performers, and those who begin with some knowledge, skills and abilities can become even better, and they and their schools and organizations will become more productive and more successful.

However, one more thing is necessary for effective performance evaluation. We should get rid of the four major drivers of individual competition: comparing employee performances against other employees; forced ranking; placing blame; and criticizing performance.

Comparing Employee Performance

Most organizations evaluate performance by comparing an employee's performance against the performance of other employees in the same department. But that can only be fair if performance standards are the same in every department. If not, there is likely to be more than one measure of "excellence," as demonstrated in the following example:

As the new Director of Human Resources, Fred was trying to familiarize himself with the company's performance evaluation system.

One form, used for evaluating production-level employees, asked managers to evaluate key performance criteria like Quantity of Work, Quality of Work, and Attendance, on a scale from 1 to 10. But what level of performance qualified as a 1, or 7, or 10 was left to each manager's discretion.

While reviewing some completed evaluation forms, Fred noticed that one manager had written "Excellent employee. Hasn't missed a day or been late in the past 4 years," but then rated that person's attendance as a 7. Confused, Fred asked the manager, "Why wouldn't a person with perfect attendance be rated a 10?" to which the manager replied, "In my department, nobody gets a 10." That left Fred asking himself, "Surely that isn't the way the system is supposed to work?"

Not long after that, Fred noticed a form from a different department on which the manager had commented "Excellent attendance. Only missed 8 days this year," and he had ranked the employee's attendance a 10. Naturally Fred asked the manager how an employee with 8 absences could be evaluated as a 10, to which the manager replied, "To me, anything less than 1 absence a month is excellent attendance."

Fred's next thought was, "What if these two employees happened to compare their evaluations; one with 8 absences rated a 10, the other with no absences a 7?" Obviously, they'd see it as an egregious example of unfair treatment.

So, he developed a new evaluation form that quantified each criterion. For example, the Attendance section of the form now specified how many absences would justify an evaluation of 1, or 7, or 10. Using that form, all managers would be evaluating performance against the same standard, and every employee would be measured against that standard.

Forced Ranking

Some companies compound the problem of comparing employee performance by requiring managers to force-rank their employees in order of their value to the department. A manager would rank her "best" employee #1, her "worst" employee #10 (depending on the number of employees being evaluated,) and everyone else somewhere in between. Those rankings would be used to determine the employee's wages and, ultimately, career potential. And some organizations take that system one step further, requiring that the lowest-ranked employee be fired each year. How ludicrous is that?

As you might imagine, Forced-ranking dramatically increases internal competition, and makes every department a zero-sum game in which one person's gain is another's loss.

Now put yourself in the position of a department manager. You've taken the time and effort to hire the best possible candidates, and devoted countless hours to helping them develop to be the best employees they can be. Then comes annual evaluation time, and suddenly your boss says you must fire your lowest-ranked employee, regardless of how good she may actually be. Bear in mind the lowest-ranked employee in a well- managed department may very well be better that half of the people in a department that's run by an average manager. With that in mind, how would you feel about hiring more employees, knowing you might have to terminate one of them during next year's evaluation period, regardless of how good she is?

Placing Blame

Blame should never have a role in performance evaluation, because it is a fact that every conscientious employee wants to do a good job. It's a matter of personal pride, so when something goes wrong we should assume it is not intentional. In fact, most performance problems are caused by something the employee did not have, like proper instruction, sufficient training, the right tools or raw materials, or enough time. When we hire people with the proper attitude, education and training, we should have confidence in their commitment to do good work. So when there's a problem, we should never attempt to find somebody to blame. Instead, the manager and the employee or employees involved should work together to determine what went wrong, what caused it, and what needs to be done to make sure it won't happen again.

Criticizing Performance

If we always hire conscientious employees and help them develop, performance evaluation should be viewed as an opportunity to praise them for what they've done well, and help them find ways to improve what they don't do well. In other words, performance evaluation should be designed to improve performance by helping each person develop to her highest potential, even if it makes her more sought-after by other organizations.

But some managers use performance evaluation as an opportunity to criticize their employees' performance, because they are genuinely afraid that praising people will make them expect more money. So they criticize performance to lower those expectations. That is not only a disservice to the employee but is devastating for individual and organizational morale.

Conclusion

Competition among students in schools or employees in organizations is always more negative than positive. It destroys the incentive for cooperation and teamwork and seriously damages individual, departmental and organizational morale. But all we need to do to minimize competition is measure each person's performance against a common set of standards instead of against other people, then eliminate the previously-discussed four main drivers of individual competition.

Then if we hire conscientious employees, people who want to do a good job, we can create a competition-free environment in which everyone has an equal opportunity to succeed, but not at anyone else's expense.

The antithesis of competition is cooperation. By improving how we evaluate performance, we can create a high-morale organizational environment that eliminates internal competition while maximizing cooperation and teamwork.

THE PRICE OF LOYALTY

When hired to work for an organization, we agree to an unwritten but very important understanding: that we will be loyal to our boss, no matter what. In its simplest form, that means doing whatever it takes to make the boss, the department, and the company successful. And should we ever get to the point where we feel we can no longer be loyal, we should leave.

John was a loyal employee who, by dedication and hard work, had earned a reputation that had helped him move up in the organization. In a relatively short time he had advanced from an entry-level position to his new job, as the "go to" person for a vice president. Little did he realize that, from there, he would have a ringside seat in the world of organizational politics.

John was proud of the good working relationships he had with his associates; relationships he had earned through trust, cooperation, and mutual respect. He assumed he would have similar relationships with his new counterparts, those who reported to the company's other vice presidents.

But it didn't take long to see that things would be different in his new position. Why? It seemed as long as everything was going well, he was able to work smoothly with his new associates, but whenever a crisis of any kind looked as though it might affect his department, John's vice president felt he had to get involved.

To make sure no problem was ever blamed on his department, he insisted that John pass all problems off to another department by taking it to the department's vice president, instead of solving it by working with associates at his own level. Apparently, his boss felt that elevating a problem to the corporate level would shift any blame to another vice president, thereby undercutting one of his counterparts without it being obvious that he was involved.

Personal competition exists in all organizations, but at lower levels it's likely to be relatively invisible. As an example, when a new employee who is trying to make a good first impression, works harder than his associates, they are likely to tell him, "slow down, you're making the rest of us look bad."

But at higher organization levels competition becomes more intense and more obvious, especially for those who see competition for the next promotion as a zero-sum game where, when someone wins, somebody else has to lose. John's boss's actions are an extreme example of that kind of competition. Although that kind of cutthroat competition can be found in almost any organization, it is more prevalent in some than others, largely due to an organization's culture.

In his case, it didn't take long for John to realize that his boss's campaign to climb the corporate ladder over the backs of his colleagues was likely to involve John in power-struggles between corporate officers. It's a sad fact that John's boss could very well have moved up based on his own knowledge, skills and abilities, because he had plenty of each, but for some reason he felt the need to undercut anyone he saw as a threat.

So John could see that, by participating in that process, even unwillingly, he had little to gain and a lot to lose, including his reputation and possibly his career. So what should he do? Normally, in this kind of dilemma, a person has three basic choices: loyalty, voice, or exit.

John knew what his boss wanted him to do was not ethical, and if he followed those orders he would probably lose self-esteem, self-respect, and possibly the respect of his colleagues. So he could see that the price of unquestioned loyalty to his boss was going to be too high. He couldn't do what his boss wanted him to without sacrificing his personal values and, as a result, his pride and self-esteem, so loyalty was no longer an option. That left him with just two choices: voice and exit.

Voice would require standing up to his boss; telling him he doesn't feel right about what the bass wants him to do, and why. Whether or not that would have any effect depends on how receptive his boss is to opinions other than his own. If the boss has a history of welcoming other opinions, telling him how he feels may be a good option. But if his boss doesn't tolerate disagreement, voice probably would not work, in which case John's only remaining option would be exit.

Exit can be the most difficult choice, because it requires finding another job, either inside the organization or, more likely, in another organization, and perhaps uprooting one's family. Leaving for another company becomes even more difficult the longer a person has been with his current employer and can be further complicated by where he is in his career and family life. So, when concerns like debt, family illnesses, or children in college make it difficult to risk job security, even exit may not be an acceptable course of action. And if even this, the last of the three options, won't work, what's left?

One possibility would be to make one more attempt at voice; try to persuade his boss to let him try another approach. If that doesn't work, and he doesn't feel he can risk leaving the company at this time, John might have no choice but to bite his tongue, sit back, and patiently try to be as loyal as he can, meanwhile hoping he can hang on until the situation changes. But wait; there is one more thing he could do: develop a backup plan for what to do if the situation doesn't change or doesn't change soon enough. Here's a real-world example:

Reporting to a boss he couldn't respect had made William miserable in his job, but he wasn't in a position to leave the company or risk losing his job. After considering what, if any, alternatives he might have, he developed a backup plan for an alternate source of income, which he decided would be real estate sales. Earning a sales license would give him something to fall back on in the event he lost his job, or his job situation finally became unbearable. So he began taking a real-estate sales class in the evenings, and by the time he had earned his license, a new sense of job security had increased his self-confidence, reduced his frustration and stress level, and generally helped ease his mind. But before he reached the point at which he felt it necessary to put the next step of his plan into action, his boss left the company, relieving him of the necessity of giving up his job.

So, although the cost of loyalty can be very high, in terms of frustration, loss of self-esteem, and personal stress, it's important to know that we don't have to live under those conditions. There are always other options. The moral of the story: although we owe the boss our loyalty, sometimes the price of loyalty can be too high. Loyalty is a two-way street: in addition to being loyal to someone else, it is important that we remain loyal to ourselves; to our personal values, pride, and self-esteem. So we should never remain loyal to someone else if that means being disloyal to ourselves. What can we do when there's a conflict of loyalties?

If we can't be loyal to the boss without being disloyal to ourselves, we can either voice our disagreement with the boss or leave, or both.

But no matter how much you disagree with your boss, or how little respect you have for him, never, under any circumstances, undercut him or discuss his shortcomings with anyone else. Either be totally loyal, or leave; there is no in-between.

Essays

Favorite Toys
By Eva Hahn

During the Christmas shopping season, I walk through the toy aisles, shaking my head in despair. All these toys and very few with any long- term play value. They will be opened, used a few times, broken, then tossed into the trash. There are very few that will be used day after day, and nothing much that will teach life skills. And even fewer that will be loved and appreciated for years.

I began to think about what toy my brothers and sisters loved. Which toys did my children use and play with for years and didn't want me to get rid of? How did the toys influence them for life? I think the toy manufactures would not like my conclusions.

Our best and most loved and most influential toy was… drum roll, please… Dirt! Dirt in one of its many forms. Dirt in the flowerpots, dirt in the form of sand, in piles and boxes, sand bars in rivers and miles of sandy beaches, dirt in construction piles, dirt under the porch, in the gardens and the cornfields and ditches near the house. Dirt became even more magical and wonderful when mixed with water. It became building material for "little people villages'" and molded into cups and cans to become flowers for castles in the sand. Ditches dug and filled with water became rivers directed with the touch of our fingers. Dirt dug out of the garden, and thrown into the ditch in front of the house during a rainstorm, became a dam, that formed a lake, that all the children in the neighborhood waded through, ran their bikes and trikes through and would become a churning mud filled swimming pool full of children, whose clothes were stained brown.

Mud of the right consistency could be molded by budding artists into little plates and cups. Future gourmet cooks filled those dishes with food formed from mud, leaves and grass. This is all before they invented play dough. Dirt near construction sites became ramps used to launch our bikes into the air, years before we ever saw "Evel Knievel" try it, resulting in many cuts and scrapes.

Summer vacation encouraged developing engineering talents, and more complex projects took form. Tunnels were dug under the straw stack at the bottom of the garden. The clover field south of the garden became a source of blocks to build a soddie at the edge of the orchard, complete with windows and doors and a fireplace for a secret fire built out of sight of mom's kitchen window.

A freshly plowed field became a track, with paths beaten down with the bare feet of several children running over them for hours at a time playing a summer version of "Fox and Goose". The farmer probably thought it strange that he had areas of the field that would grow nothing. Summer rains turned a bare spot in the middle of the yard into a muddy "slip and slide." After hours of play my boys returned to the house coated in mud from head to toe, with the only clean spot on them being the inside of their eyelids and inside of their lips. Clean up required a complete hosing down outside and clothes soaked in a bucket. Mud on the side of a river, creek or ditch became a water slide made faster with each bucket of water poured down it. Since mother hid her garden trowel so it wouldn't disappear, budding engineers used the handiest tool they had access to; Mom's spoons. The number in the drawer would dwindle until mom would go to a rummage sale or store to replenish her supply. Bent, broken, lost and damaged spoons were always turning up in the garden or sand pile.

Using a spoon, my bored nephew began to dig a hole in the backyard. It grew deeper each day until it was two feet square and two feet deep. Then his stepfather gave him a shovel to use and by the end of the summer the hole became a storm shelter complete with a concrete floor and walls.

Our family had produced engineers, coal miners, gardeners, potters, carpenters, landscapers, artist and other occupations that involve getting dirty. I can't help thinking the sand, dirt, mud, water and left-over construction materials we played with as children had a great influence on the paths we chose as adults.

Getting into the High Bed

Eva Hahn

Margaret didn't speak until age three.
Then my little sister's words astonished me,
Words no three-year-old should know.
"I am not going to grow up.
I am going to die and go to heaven."

Others thought it strange Over and over asking her,
"What are you going to be when you grow up?"

She said, "Nothing…"
Death stood in the doorway, listening,
Planning how to fulfill her words.
As a great predator after the weak and the young,
It began to stalk her.

Margaret protected and cared for others
Like a sheep dog guarding the flock,
Guiding the baby back to the house
When he followed mom to the barn, or
Urging Daddy up the stairs when he drank too much.

Death moved in closer
When she found the bottle of acid under the porch.
Evil was contained within, and
Like Pandora's Box when opened,
It leapt out to get her, burning her legs.

Daddy was moving furniture that day.
She asked to sit in the bed of the truck.
And as he backed to park it,
Her eyes saw the toddler coming off the porch,
Down the steps, into the path of danger.
"Go back, go back!" she said.
And as she stood, she hit her head.

Now death was near digging its claws into her,
like the crawdad she had found

In the mud under the house.
It grabbed her by the hand
And hung on, refusing to let go.

Her head was cradled in Mom's arms
As they rushed her to the hospital.
Everyone told me she would be fine,
"She'll be home in a few days."

In the hospital, as pneumonia took hold,
Margaret said to Mom and Dad,
"I'm not getting better,
I'm getting into that high bed."

They held the wake at home.
They moved furniture from our bedroom,
The casket was placed in the corner.
She lay so still on her high bed.
I asked, "How could she be gone,
Never to play with me again?"

We said prayers at the cemetery,
And as we turned to walk away, I asked,
"Who will sleep with me? I will be so lonely."
Death heard and crawled in bed with me
Bringing fears to keep me cowering.
Dark forms came to invade my dreams
Of death taking my parents hostage.

Loneliness came to enclose me in a glass bell jar.
Keeping me in, others out,
"Don't get close...
Look, don't touch." Allowing no one in.

I was seven and my sister Margaret was four and a half-years old
when she died of pneumonia, three days after receiving a concussion
to her head. They did not let children into the hospital to visit, so
the last time I saw my sister alive was as they put her into the car to
rush her to the hospital.

In the Heat of the Night
Eva Hahn

Sleep doesn't come when your body and hair are soaked in sweat. The hot damp body of my little sister, so welcome and snuggly in the winter, becomes a hot sticky bundle to be avoided and kept at arm's length. I want her to stay on her own side of her bed and not try to touch me with her toes. Even hot air moving across my body feels cool. Beads of sweat on my forehead remind me to turn my face toward the window fan. I pick up my pillow and turn it over to the cool side, the one not full of my body heat. I move my toes out across the sheets, searching to find a spot where the fabric feels cool and smooth against my feet. I toss and turn waiting for the outside air to drop a few degrees so the fan can draw it in and wash over my shoulders until I can finally pull the top sheet over me, curl into a sleeping position and nod off until the early morning sun warms up my bedroom.

Some chores are best done in the early morning before the dew evaporates. Weeds in the garden seem to come out easier. The blades of the cornstalks are not so sharp, and the dust and pollen do not stick to my skin like they do later in the day's heat. The green beans picked in the morning's cool can be snapped as I sit in the shade of the big pecan tree talking to mom or my sisters. My brothers argue over who must carry the corn shucks to the cow and what must be done before they can go to the river for a swim. Carrying water to the chickens on a hot afternoon is a rather pleasant chore. The chill from the bottom of the well seems to escape along with the water filling the bucket. Before I start to the hen house, I splash some water over my arms and face washing off the dirt and itchy weeds. As the bucket hits against my leg, the water slops out and over my bare feet, cooling my whole body. Maybe a swim in the river with my brothers before bed will make it easier to sleep tonight.

Memories

Eva Hahn

Memories crowd forward,
Out of dark closets,
Asking me to stop and listen.
Whispering in my ear, tugging at my sleeve.

Like a group of kindergartners at Show and Tell,
Each one begging to be chosen.
"Me! Me! Choose me. Let me tell my story,
Give me a voice. Choose me, please."

Some remind me of their importance,
While others stay shyly back, waiting…
With fear in their eyes,
That they will be forgotten.

Others come from my granddaughter,
Snuggled up next to me,
Asking for stories of her mommy
When she was little.
Memories, waiting to be heard…
Asking for a voice
Sneaking up on me
Unexpected
Asking to be tasted
Like "Old Country" soup

Prisoners of War

Eva Hahn

They were boys who loved to hunt and fish
Boys who love to read and study
Boys who loved the farm
Boys who loved the girls back home.
They were boys who worked on cars,
Who married and had wives.
They answered the call of their country,
A call that would change their lives.

They were taught about war
But nothing could prepare them for
What they saw and heard and the grief they bore,
As they saw others around them fall,
Friends who also answered the call.

They came back to us to sleep in our beds
With nightmarish images filling their heads
Of incoming rockets and faces of the dead.
Dreams that filled them full of fear,
Sounds that no one else could hear.

Some were damaged and broken on the outside,
Others drenched in Agent Orange
That would kill them just the same.
Some filled with anger, hate and grief,
And turned to alcohol and drugs to find relief.

Some were not maimed on the outside
But war had tainted their souls,
And flashbacks came to haunt them,
Of young soldiers, sons, husbands and fathers
With body parts missing, charred by napalm.
Body bags lined in rows ready to go home.

Staring and silent, afraid to share
They filled psych units everywhere
Suicide took some, others withdrew

Had panic attack and restless pacing
Terrifying nightmares, hands constantly shaking.
Restless, homeless, amputees
Wandered the streets of the cities
Sleeping under bridges, in old cars
Staying in shelters, hanging out in bars
They had answered the call of their country
Boys who answered the call returned as men
Who fought a war they couldn't win.
Who never spent a night in the Hanoi Hilton,
Yet in their bodies and minds
They were prisoners of war.

She Never Opened Them

Eva Hahn

There she goes, slipping out of our little country church as soon as communion is over before the final blessing. My mother's Aunt Evelyn never stayed to talk or visit after church. She always slipped out the back door and was halfway across the yard ready to disappear from site down the path that ran between the woods and cornfield. All we could see was a glimpse of her coattails flying in the wind. She wore a scarf tied around her head. It knotted and tucked into the back, so nothing showed. None of us had ever seen even a wisp of hair, so the children thought she was bald under the knotted headscarf. My mother told me that a nephew from Missouri dared to ask her if she was bald. She flew into a rage and forbade him to come to her house again.

She looked like the wicked Witch of the West from the Wizard of Oz, with a sharp nose and piercing eyes that made children squirm. Her skirts were long, dark and old. In the summer, she perched a straw hat over her covered head. In the winter, she wore old gloves with holes in the fingers. She replaced her summer straw hat with a man's hat with fur lined flaps worn down over her ears. Her coat was long and ragged looking, matching her Witch of the West image.

Her husband, Uncle George, was just the opposite. He had a full head of white hair and mustache and a wonderful smile and looked like my grandpa Ochs. He hung around and visited after church, then walked down to the gravel towards home. If we went to visit at their house Uncle George would show off all the tricks of his fat old beagle, Jack. He would also show us the picture of Jack, whose eyes followed us no matter where we were in the room.

Aunt Evelyn was talkative in her own environment, showing off her garden and flowers. They lived in the basement of their home. I never thought much about it, since several of our neighbors lived in their basement while their house was being built or remodeled.

I left for college, and during these years my mother told me that uncle George had died, and neighbors were helping Aunt Evelyn out, taking her shopping, paying her bills, and taking her to the doctor's appointments. While I was raising my brood, Evelyn died. They had no children, so the neighbor who had been farming the ground, bought the house and land. He would sell the contents of the house at auction. The ladies of the neighborhood volunteered to get the house cleaned out and ready.

They cleaned out the basement where Aunt Evelyn lived. When they started on the ground floor, they found a path they could not open only wide enough for a tiny woman and the doors of the bedrooms more than a few inches. Reaching through the narrow gap they began to remove things. There were boxes of old cereals, bags of canned goods, groceries of every kind. Most of them were old and had expired.

The other bedroom was filled with boxes of wrapped gifts, bows and ribbons still in place. Never opened. As the ladies began to open the boxes, they discovered beautiful, warm, comfortable sweaters, neat blouses, and colorful skirts and dresses. Other boxes revealed warm jackets, winter coats, scarves of every color and warm knitted mufflers. There were also wrapped sets of mittens and women's hats; all new, all wrapped, all unopened. Gifts given to her for birthdays, anniversaries, Christmas and, "Just thought you might like this," times. Gifts from friends, relatives and neighbors, who wondered why she never wore them. Gifts from those who saw a need and bought what they thought would please her. Gifts accepted, but never, never used, never even admired.

I began to wonder, meditate, contemplate, ask myself, "How many gifts have I accepted from God, friends and family, that I have never opened, never used, never tried on for size, never developed?" I don't want my epitaph to read, "She never opened them"

Why Do I Write

Eva Hahn

I am like a pond on a quiet day. The surface is still. No ripples or disturbances are apparent. If you stand at the edge of the water, you never know what is beneath the surface.

I write to invite you to come closer; to take off your shoes and wade in, and to feel the coolness and mud between your toes. Sit down and let the water engulf you; allow your eyes to look around. Darting under the surface, minnows come out of hiding to investigate your fingers and your toes, and if you stay still a blue gill or bass will follow, edging in, and hoping for a meal.

I write because I am like that pond, appearing very calm on the surface, but full of the experiences of life. The dramas of life keep coming in close to me, causing disturbances deep in the water. Life keeps showing me pictures that only words can explain. I write as a warning, so others do not have to follow the same path I trod, unless they choose to.

I write because words are powerful. They inform, sway and frighten. They create with many colors, shades and textures. Words allow others to come close and to share my thoughts, feeling and emotions, my very soul. Though you stand right next to me, you cannot know me unless my words open the door to you, inviting you in.

Reading and writing is a privilege not available to everyone. Invading armies closed all the schools in my grandfather's country, so they denied him any chance for an education. Because he could not write his name, an immigration official determined the spelling of our family name, and none of his life story was written down. So, I write to pass on a legacy of experiences, stories and history

---

A Shift in Humanity

Carley Mattimore

It has been disheartening, frustrating and even traumatizing to witness the reversals of our hard-won efforts to bring balance and equality to our social and political systems.

A new consort of players is at the helm of these reversals of the protection of the rights of people, animals and nature. The laws being dismantled were ones that protected our civil rights, women's rights, eco- system, natural forests, endangered species such as grizzly bears, wolves and elephants to name a few.

People in positions of power in our political realm, whose actions are affecting all of humanity, are making decisions that relegate animals to the status of non-conscious beings. These mandates are reversing the progress made in the last few years, especially since the killing of Cecil the Lion in Zimbabwe, that protected animals, especially endangered animals, from being killed for sport or trophies.

This recent pushback is the effort of the old patriarchal system to hang on to the hierarchical beliefs of separation between nature and humans, between all who are labeled "other" and themselves, a model developed out of fear of the feminine, of inclusion, vulnerability, connection and of love itself.

This old model has been around for a long time, and is based on the Cartesian model of science and the reductionist concept of the "rational." It evolved as a model of detachment from emotion, intuition, compassion and interconnection; traits that we as a civilization have associated with the feminine. These traits were suppressed, creating a belief that humans were superior to nature; and that white males were superior to women, people of color, animals and the natural environment (water, trees, earth, minerals, etc.). Dominance over the "other" develops when there is fear. The longer it lasts the more the fear grows, until it is not even conscious anymore. Imagine thinking about something you avoid doing—the longer you avoid it the bigger it gets and the more fear is attached to it. At the same time you become more detached from the original event; pushing it down, internalizing it so it becomes embedded into the
unconscious realms of your own shadow.

In this place, we keep it down until something triggers it and it comes forth as a projection onto someone else, which is what happens when we can't see something in ourselves because we buried it. Think of how we avoid dealing with an uncomfortable issue and refuse to talk to a family member, old boss or friend—someone we feel hurt us. The longer we avoid dealing with the problem, the more distanced we become from the pain, ignoring it until it is deeply buried in our psyche.

This buried shadow aspect is something that occurs not just in individuals but also in societies; we bury the wound, closing a door over the hurt, justifying wrapping it up in layers of avoidance because the story we make up about it is so painful. We try to keep it stuffed but it takes a lot of energy, like holding a beach ball under water. This happens in society too as we are a collective of ideas, beliefs and patterns that over time form an overarching belief of the times. These beliefs are referred to as a paradigm; a worldview of the era.

Paradigms change eventually, as we are organic living beings constantly evolving our understanding of our world as we digest our experiences. As individuals we change our perception of things as we grow from children to adults, our view expanding from what we have learned from our experiences, so that we see with new eyes. What I believed when I was twenty, thirty or sixty is not what I believe now and that is because my experiences have shaped me, giving me more depth and breadth to challenge those old stories about my world.

This happens for society too; as new information and new experiences come into our awareness we become ready to challenge an old belief system or view of the world. It can be seen as the world becoming ready to heal something that it has repressed, something that no longer serves humanity, the old pain that can no longer be held under water like a beach ball. It is forcing its way up to be healed and transformed, to bring forth a deeper, richer understanding and meaning for us.

In 1979 in a Systems Theory Psychology class at a small well-regarded religious college I attended in the Midwest, we were required to read The Structure of Scientific Revolutions by Thomas Kuhn. I remember reading and digesting its wisdom, getting a new understanding of how theories in science, including psychology, can be replaced as new evidence comes into play that challenges the current belief system, and how defenders of the old paradigm ignore or deny the evidence that is under their noses.

These are referred to as radical paradigm shifts; a belief system formerly substantiated by scientific evidence collapses as new evidence is gathered that gives a different, sometimes radically different, understanding.

To move to a new paradigm, we must go through a cycle of death and rebirth; the old has to metaphorically die as we know it before it can come into new form. This process simulates the birth process of gestation (Water cycle), moving down the birth canal (Earth), transition (Fire), surrender (Spirit) and birth (Air). We are cycling through this process over and over again, both at a personal and collective level. It is how change happens.

It is a process of change that aligns with the Cycles of Change and Spiral Path model developed by Linda Star Wolf. Personally, and collectively we move through change on a spiral continuum revisiting an issue but at a higher octave of understanding. We move towards higher levels of consciousness.

However, even with the impulse to grow there is often fear and great resistance seen in those who are the defenders of the status quo. The old ways hang on, clinging to the old model, belief system or power, afraid to let go because the fear of change manifests in a struggle for control. So they deny the changes that are very much right in their face.

This is so obvious to many right now and we see it expressed in many ways that stun us in their level of denial. The movement to deny that animals are sentient beings and that they do not feel pain or have consciousness is in direct opposition to the overwhelming documented information available to us now through movies, video clips, photographs, scientific research, etc., of animals displaying behaviors of compassion and friendship between species and across species; behaviors we used to believe were only possessed by humans. It is clear that animals show compassion, respect, knowledge and complex thinking and engage with each other in complex and supportive ways.

It is imperative that we act with courage to overcome the efforts of those whose fear causes them to attempt to block this new paradigm— the new relationship with the feminine. This requires each of us to stand in the conviction of our own "inner knowing," to embody a deeper understanding of our interconnectedness and interdependence and protect what has meaning and value to our survival as a civilization. This requires us to take action and to stand by the principle that animals are sentient beings who are far more evolved than our previous paradigm suggested.

This new paradigm includes a deep reverence for all of life

---

including animals, plant life and humans of all orientations whether it be gender, race, religion, socio-economic status…each of us is a part of the whole. We are bringing together a deeper understanding and the healing of the false separation from the "other"; between our right and left-brain traits, and embodying our healthy traits of focused action with intuition and heart. It is time for us to stand as lion-hearted leaders in a world that seeks to return to a time of love and respect for each other including non-human beings who have so much to teach us.

Pain or Pleasure

Teri Freesmeyer

Pain or pleasure?

Love or war? Peace or struggle? Feast or famine? Duality in our world can end. We can do something about it. Whether a business tycoon motivated in greed, an unschooled housewife motivated by exhaustion, a blue-collar dame determined to equalize her work or a busboy with no sleep hungrily auditioning for the stage. Whoever you are on the planet, duality in our world can end; it begins with our inner world. A few simple steps on the path to awareness as we move through our day can thin the veil of mass consciousness that affects our inner perceptions of pain or pleasure; reaction to action.

We must begin to feel consciously. To be in the body instead of just the mind tumbling absently with emotion is the beginning to an end. As we move into the awareness of what is going on, what is the core of our discomfort, going deeper into our emotions we find those parts of ourselves we have disconnected from. When resistance or fear rages, we look into it; face it head on and see what is standing behind it. What part of us needs acknowledged? Who is within needing embraced?

We continue to have emotions and react to them, hide them away "thinking" that will make it go away or we don't have time to look at that. No worries, it will rear its ugly head again and give you another chance.

This is it folks. This is why we are here; to feel. To feel we must be in our body. And often because we feel, we have left the body. So many excuses the unconscious stutters. It doesn't always feel good in there. "It's not safe. We are alone. Unloved. Afraid of our power. Filled with self-loathing. Upset. Aching or broken hearted. Stuck in the muck. We have tried to love and failed. We have received love and gotten hurt." Oh, the list goes on and on to the reasons we abandon ourselves and our feelings.

Abandonment is but one of the many reasons.

To every action there is a reaction, to every emotion there is an emotion. Our thoughts run rampant and sometimes aren't even our thoughts. Our feelings are our own unique treasures. Yes you can feel another's feelings, but how they show up in you is like your own unique snowflake on the ground of your being. And these precious particles of the human experience are also the components that make love and war, feast or famine, peace or struggle a possibility. The duality of emotions, good or bad does not exist when we are balanced in what is there.

Yet we skim over what is there mostly due to past or future. When we are present with what is there, how we feel, who we are at war, struggle or pain with, where that feeling is IN OUR BODY, we can find the how to balance it.

*I can help. I am a storyteller of the body. I can help you discover the great treasure of you that lies or lies within you. Through bodywork, energy work, coaching, and intuitive healing practice I customize your session or sessions to self-discover, self-heal, as a supportive and integrative spiritual counsel to unveil the clouds of conflict and confusion keeping you from knowing and embracing the YOU.

You are here to experience. Every brilliant cell, each dazzling pound, every nuance of hair, bone, tissue and teeth. Become aware of those grasping thoughts and beliefs that serve and support. Relinquish those buried in last year's WAR-drobe of slight imperfections. Ready to love more fully, manifest more prosperity, excel in your excellence, or find peace in your being.....call me.

The Mandela Effect is BS

Keri Goble Billick

I recently heard an episode of Radiolab (This one: http://www.radiolab. org/story/91569-memory-and-forgetting/) which talked about memory and how it works. I found it very compelling and, as sometimes happens with these things, it got me to thinking. But let me take a step back first. I have an intense dislike for the recent internet obsession with something that has come to be known as the Mandela Effect. In case you have been binge watching stuff instead of breezing through the FaceBook
or watching the YouTubes, I can give you a brief summary of it.

In 2010 Fiona Broome launched a website in which she used the phrase "the Mandela Effect." She used it to describe an emerging phenomenon she had noticed (her words). It is, basically, when someone has a very clear memory of something that never happened or happened differently than they recall. Broome took it one step further and posted that it was something that never happened or happened differently in this reality.

The concept has blown up. It is everywhere and almost everyone is talking about it, has read about it or is actually experiencing it. Perhaps you yourself remember talk of a Sinbad movie called Shazam that people remember or people swearing Darth Vader said, "Luke, I am your father." Instead of "No, I am your father." If not, go do a YouTube search for Mandela Effect and be entertained for hours.

The thing is, it's all horse feathers. It's all hooey. It's all a hot steaming pile of.. well, you get the point. It is basically a very creative way to explain misremembering things. Coupled with the internet and the ability to instantly share observations and get immediate validation of an idea (even a misremembered one) it has grown to this "phenomenon" Fiona Broome coined.

I could rail on and on about how it doesn't make sense at a base level. How it is far more likely (Occam's razor) that people simple don't remember things correctly than an after effect of CERN messing with protons and accidentally breaching other dimensions which are slowly leaking into our reality and changing things right under our noses. How any belief in the topic or engagement going deeper than poking fun at the extreme premises, debunking it or joining in on making up possible scenarios for giggles is tin foil hat crazy.

I   could.

And have.

But this little collection of words is to give a more scientific based explanation for the "phenomenon" rather than a science fiction based one. And the inspiration for this explanation was that episode of Radiolab about memory. It was really good, I highly recommend it.

In it the hosts interviewed Joe LeDoux and others in his field regarding research of what goes into creating and recalling a memory. He began his research in the 1960's. Scientists had discovered a drug called anisomycin. Also called flagecidin, it is an antibiotic which inhibits eukaryotic protein synthesis.

But Keri, what is the big deal about inhibiting eukaryotic protein synthesis, you ask? Good question, and I am glad you asked it. The properties of the drug enabled scientists to prove that memory is constructed in our brains from proteins. Without going into a ton of detail (listen to the podcast) the drug induces amnesia. They did studies with rats to find out why. In these experiments and studies they were able to identify how memory is written in our brains. No rats were seriously harmed or killed in this research.

Memory is a structure which connects one brain cell to another brain cell. This connection is made of protein. In the experiment they used anisomycin on the rats at the exact moment a memory was being formed. The drug inhibited the generation of the proteins and the memory wasn't formed. It proves that the memory link is made of protein.

Conversely, once the memory is in there, and built, it is a done deal. The connection is there. The drug can't remove it after the fact. All of that is way cool to know, but the next steps of the research were even cooler. They wanted to see what would happen if they used the drug while the memory was being accessed. What they learned was that doing this removed the memory altogether.

I'll let that sink in.

If it is timed right, using this drug when you access a memory removed the memory from your brain. For example. Let's say I accidentally gave you a spoiler and told you that Glen and Abraham died in the premier of season 7 of TWD. After you were all, "NO KERI, WHY DID YOU TELL ME THAT?!?" we could fix it. If we administered the drug while you remembered who died in the episode you would forget. The link that enabled that memory would no longer exist.

I know that is a lot to process and the implications even more so.

It means that when we remember something, we are both accessing the memory via the proteins and at the same time re-constructing the protein bridge to maintain the memory further. It becomes a brand-new memory. Sort of a rebooted version of the original memory, evolving over time.

It gets way more complicated with time. Each time you access and re-write a memory you also build other bridges between cells and create new pathways to access the memory. In our example, you like Michael Cudlitz, the actor who played Abraham. You associate the character both with the storyline and the actor. When we eliminate the spoiler the protein pathway isn't recreated regarding the storyline, but the pathway regarding the actor is still there. The next time you watch Gross Point Blank it comes back to you that Abraham will die in the series premier of season 7 and you call me up to yell at me.

Ongoing research has led to a greater understanding of how false memories can be built or implanted. In addition, anisomycin could be used therapeutically to help reduce the stressful impact of traumatic memories. But, uses of the knowledge and drug aside, it means that what we remember is re-created every time we remember it. The implications of this reality are what got me thinking about the Mandela Effect.

What I am saying, essentially, is that the biology of how memory works is at fault for the Mandela Effect. Poor education, political propaganda, charismatic stories, similarity in content and a billion other factors can impact our memory of facts or events. When we recreate a memory the introduction of the possibility that it has been changed by fantastic factors is causing the memory to change. Naming the mistaken memory and creating an unprovable scientific (ish) reason for it is just a complicated denial of the fact that you aren't remembering it as it happened. Other people misremembering it in the same way isn't proof you are all right, it is proof you all read the same articles on the internet and don't understand how memory works.

I realize this is an argument that will never fly with the true believers. You can lead a horse to water but you can't make it believe that there isn't a breakdown in dimensional boundaries rewriting our history because of CERN trying to save us from the end of the world that happened in some realities in 2012. The irony of the "phenomenon" is that the "proof" many believers will provide to convince us that history is being re-written is likely the catalyst for the change in their memories to begin with.

The Mandela Effect is complete and utter fiction.

Except for the Sally Field Oscar acceptance speech. That shit is real.

www.ingramcontent.com/pod-product-compliance
Lightning Source LLC
Chambersburg PA
CBHW071324250626
47159CB00004B/1447